JENNIFER, NADINE, VICTORIA AND PSYCHOKINETIC TELEPATHY

JENNIFER, NADINE, VICTORIA AND PSYCHOKINETIC TELEPATHY

A.J. PRINCE

authorHOUSE®

AuthorHouse™
1663 Liberty Drive
Bloomington, IN 47403
www.authorhouse.com
Phone: 1-800-839-8640

First published by AuthorHouse   05/17/2011

ISBN: 978-1-4634-0637-0 (sc)
ISBN: 978-1-4634-0636-3 (ebk)

Library of Congress Control Number: 2011908262

Printed in the United States of America

Contents

Vocabulary

DP = Direct perception

DC = direct communication

DE = direct experience

CL = complete life

IL = incomplete life

HBB = human being becoming

TBs = transcendental behaviors

Chapter 1

<u>INTRODUCTION</u>

How It Started?

After having been wrongfully dismissed as a teacher on call in Delta School Board in 1991, I decided to still looking for a new job at the same time to make research in parapsychology field in order to be able to create my goals. In 1997, not finding paying full time work as such I started the research in télépathy.

First of all I wanted to just communicate with tithe subjects and find out that if they have consciousness of the telepathic communication. Wanting to push the research a bit further, later, I add to that they will call me to tell me that they have received my telepathic message and that they are letting me know.

That is why part of the title is psychokinetic telepathy and. According to the results the telepathic part succeeds.

The same cannot be said about the psychokinetic part (to call) probably because I was to present in the research by having a goal in mind. While the good rational way is to have a broad idea in mind and let the phenomenon takes it wherever is necessary. However it did take me ways I did not expected.

There has been research on telepathy and psychokinetic event at universities in United States of America and in Yugoslavia. They researchers did send message to subjects in Yugoslavia. They did receive the messages (What Universities?). It was a research made in laboratory I find them too skimpy and that to ground the phenomenon we need more than that, more than Very light statistics (unfinished).

My interest in psychology started probably a few years after I was born, being alone to chew on the death of our mother and not wanting to live close by half families. I started by taking a few psychology classes at the University of Quebec in Montreal, while studying to get certificate in Education, I kept learning psychology since then, alone as a free lance researcher.

OBSERVING AND QUESTIONING OUR CREATOR=UNIVERSAL SELF

I was interested in dream very far back, however, having problems with a stable employment, it came to me to have goals and the means to create them. In psychology the major ones are meditation and yoga. I try meditation, I was not satisfied with it probably because it is better to do it during the day, and who has time during the day, looking for work, doing one job or another. I did not try meditation during the night. I was commuting from Vancouver to Abbottsford to go to teach there in the car I was driving at that time. I was falling asleep while driving the car. Meditation had certainly something to do with it at night one would be too tired to do meditation without falling asleep during the sessions. I was not familiar with yoga. I chose to create the goals by dream which I called direct perception, which takes only a few wakes up at night to do.

By Recording many DPs with which I wrote the Soul Exposed, and by reading many books especially Mindfulness by Heidegger I discovered that all the time I was observing, questioning Sophia in order to ground its truth by working with DPs. I had to record my Dips to get ideas from them because things were not going right in my life the same way it is not going well right in the world of pollution and violence. We are ideally bankrupted, left to our own, turning our back to our Creator. The result is a lack of ideas the reason why we keep repeating history, creating the same cars the same houses the same technologies, making the same mistakes again and again

The earth is being savagely destroyed. I am not a fanatic in anything, however the destruction is the consequence of a lack of new ideas. We can continue like that for a while but ultimately we run the possibility of destroying ourselves. With our Creator we can have it all without Reality we have nothing, not even ourselves. For staying away from the creator we run the risk of being the object of entropy, the physical law that says that anything left to itself will be taken over by nature, will be in a state of bits and pieces, parallel to death.

In the news recently it was question of system of sit belt and cushion bag in cars replaced by a new one but the new one performs less than the old one. We are running after the new things without consideration if of a better performance, we are running after the new just because they are new. In the news recently (To day is 30-03-2010) there was also the scandal about alleged sexual abuse on children in the catholic churches involving the pope in cover-up.

Everyone is doing his best in life. The mechanic person is fixing cars, the plumbers are unblocking water pipes. Meaning that the priests and the pope are doing church work. The problem starts with us, it seems, when we are applying bad ideas from bad principles, bad theory. I am thinking of the occidental metaphysics started from Plato, wrongly translated by Hegel and Nitzsche from which religious personalities draw their ideas. Absolute reason, absolute body, ultimate consciousness, and all in all animal spirit.

We do not have to have university degree to know that sexually abusing children does not sound right, to understand that the individuals doing these sorts of thing are not inspired by reason, by real science, to realize that in the theory they are applying is the seeds for sexually abusing children. In the Whole that is what we get in the field of unscientific faith, children abusers. That exists in the society at large too, however no one expects it in church.

Advaita Vedanta, an Indian teacher who teaches the essential unity of each individual with the Universal Consciousness (I supposed he is referring the Creator) and Krishnameurti consider Christianity as being an inferior religion (we can add to that Heidegger's reflection "Christian religion thinking not adequate, it is propagandist construct to keep the dogma alive). Close inside of metaphysics wall it is unlikely they are going to get out of such disqualification. We have to admit that that kind of disqualification goes as well for science without faith, There too metaphysics reign with strong claws on scientific thinking. Obviously we need scientific spirituality. Strangely enough Vedanta and Krishnamerti were already of this kind of spirituality or this kind of science, although I am not completely thinking like them, given that they have the concept of Universal Consciousness while I have in Mind Universal Self or Reality or the Creator.

This situation is not better in the field of sciences where newness at all price, exacting, actualizing—"where actualizing no longer grasped as the presencing of the constant, but as the actual action, the power of effectiveness, the power and the powerful" as said Heidegger—effectiveness for what is immediately useful, the presencing are the paradigm of all times. In other words we have a science without faith.

Nothing permanent, useful, authenticating human life will come from unscientific faith, neither from unfaithful science. We need to observe our Creator in order to ground its truth (I started the research in and psychokinetic telepathy in the same state of mind). I am not against anything as such, but I am for, our Creator. I am promoting our Creator who seems to have been dumped by us to our risks and perils. There is no dogma in the Reality I am promoting, for observing it and grounding Its truth mean exactly that truth will be your truth so different of mine, of others.

There is no particular religion in that promotion although according to archetypal psychology religiosity is universal activity in the sense that it is a feature of human character, that is, we all do religion somehow.

Recently I saw what I think is the Creator again in a DP It was in my room or I felt its presence in my room. I started to complain about the long period of time it takes me doing the observation without creating any goals yet. Then I try to approach it and touch It a few times. It escaped each time and appears at another place in the room. It was a beautiful orange colored thing or light, in other DPs I saw a woman passing by me, I tried to touch her hand. She pulled her hand from mine abruptly. Reality (can appear to us in many forms, thing, animals, men and women) is not to be kept, not to be approached not to be touched according to what they say and my DP experiences.

Another time in a DP I saw a woman I used to see in a couple DPs before wearing a white robe on a horse. For me the horse symbolizes nature, so the being I saw in my room was supposed to be goddess of nature, dame nature in French. Then later a small man appeared in the room and penetrated the woman under my eyesight with a long penis. I think in some mythic belief what happened in my room supposed to make me an initiate in the divine field and that when that happened in a room the room becomes sacred. However it is according to a myth. There is no way that can be proven.

The explanation that would stand the most in psychology of today what I called co-appearance of psychic and erotic consciousness, according to what I have read in archetypal psychology

Another image related to Reality is one high heel woman shoe, is it a soleto? I saw it quite often. I say it is related to reality because it is only one shoe and that I associate shoe with soul. So reality, the creator has a feminine, side to it the reason why it is also called Sophia (should rather be goddess of wisdom) in certain cultures? However, images, starting of complete life event, are related to soul, soul is not the Creator, is one of its creations.

In DP most of the time I am in total darkness. That situation would make me an occultist. Still I used DP during the research in telepathy, because, as you seen, I could not use the meditation technique. I do not think it makes me any other than myself. Anyway I am no longer living in the place where the room is. Will the new individual living in it now become initiated in divinity just because I was living there? It does not seem likely.

SELF—I—EGO

In the psychology of Today the self-concept is not really developed except in the eastern psychology where the talk is about unifying the self with the rest of life. However it still has an air of psychology of 1900 when things started to unravel in the field. Hedger even put the concept of self down. I disagree on putting the individual self-concept down for it unifies the different part of the personality and I am not talking the kind of unification in Eastern Psychology, which is a type of environmental unification with the self. The unification I mention is inner unification, which necessarily brings with it the external unification. Furthermore, the individual self-concept is a good way to understand, to connect with the Universal Self, another term for the Creator as we have seen above.

However I agree with Heideger that the focus on the individual self will bring us nowhere unless we make the link with the Universal Self and focus on the Creator more or as much as on the individual self. Since the beginning of the individual self-concept nothing has changed really in life, no progress in the spiritual level of the world has been made. Human beings are still facing too many troubles.

After we have a bit of soul, or should I say, after we activate our soul capacity, what comes next is the "I" which is the resultant of meeting of the individual soul and the Soul of the World. "I" becomes the imaginal "I" that I use to make DP. This "I" is different from the I representing the ego.

I have a strange history with the ego concept. In my first writings I talked about myself in the third person (himself instead myself). Later I utilized you instead of the I representing the ego, later again, I realized that the ego is an essential part if human being. So I was still struggling with the concept. Until recently when I started to use the concept being instead of the ego (my being instead I or me). I am satisfied now with the use being, for in it there are all my parts, my ego (containing the past, and a sense of the empirical body), my I (dealing with future, creation, imagination), my soul and my spirit. When I was using the ego, all the other parts of disappeared. The tendency in psychology is to "relativize" the ego concept, but surrounded every where by monotheism; it is something difficult to do. Even myself again today many times I want to think of my being or write it I think or write my ego in its place. It happens to me in French the equivalent term is "moi". I do not know if it would be the same in English and other languages in the world. At all cases, in English the terms I and me are equivalent to the ego most of the time.

FREEDOM

We have to eat to sleep, to have our feet on the ground all the time in order not to be flying in the space forever. We have to move other wise we would die in a matter of days, to breathe, to drink water. We could choose to die instead then we would not have anything to talk about. Furthermore it seems the dead too has limited freedom. It appears that they cannot address the living human unless the latter invoke them first so we are not totally free. Nonetheless, the fact that we can turn our back to our Creator speaks loud for the fundamentality or importance of freedom—as well as choice, refusal, valorization—the freedom we have, on that we finally the ones who choose the way our life is, to be or not be. The belief is that we make a choice even without making one, that is, we choose not to make one.

My DPs are telling me also that we are unable to make choices in our lives or we are hesitating to do them, because we do not choose our Creator, the ab-ground, or background of everything in our lives.

On the other hand freedom is responsible for all human miseries in life, for the creator would not let anything happen to us. We would not have choice but to do the right thing all the time. How would we feel living that way without being able to make a mistake? We would not have to learn to walk, to ride a bike, to go to school. We would not have to learn how to meet the opposite sex; we would not have to learn anything. The answer to the question is not easy to say. What is sure we would not have any freedom? We would not be able to turn our back to Reality. We would not be able to chose to live a frenzied life, which seems to conducing us straight to oblivion, caput, and nada.

ANIMAL SPIRIT AND ANIMAL COMMUNICATION

SPIRIT

I have read Mindfulness by Heidegger last September 2009, I practically and systematically started to observe our creator in 1991, I started the research in telepathic "psychokinetic moment" in 1997 way before I read Mindfulness The book helps me to refine my ideas on the world and Our creator. I remember having the DP during which I saw a big number of animals mostly lamb. To my great astonishment they where all talking to me. I met some in the street; some followed me in my place. I did not understand why it was like that why animals were talking to me. They were telling me about the animal spirit in metaphysics.

I did not know either in our right mind we would think of an animal spirit, that it was what metaphysics of Nietzsche and Hegel mean. As said above we all do our best, however absolute reason and absolute body make me think of absolute ceramic. They were lost in translation as the say.

COMMUNICATION

As for animal communication it is a bran new way to communicate I observed in living in shared accommodation. At first I thought it was used by homosexual uncomfortable with their life style.

Then I realized that women are using it too. The platform of that kind of communication is like domino playing. to tell someone you want to have a sexual encounter with him or her you just leave a knife or fork where the person can see it, without telling him anything. For a woman to ask you to make love with her, just comes near you smiling, sometimes not even smiling, while her husband is upstairs without telling you anything, without touching you caressingly, while you may have many problems in mind that you are trying to solve, while you may be very upset about something else that is happening in your life. Sometimes only later you realize what she was trying to communicate to you. That is what I call animal communication, without words, and any other aspect of human communication.

In my case they all fail, not only because it is from a homosexual, but also coming from a woman I like. I would say that that kind of animal communication will fail in 90% of cases to communicate an idea effectively. Because HBBs have tongue, voices and languages, they are not supposed to communicate like an animal. They are supposed to speak to communicate. When you smile at someone you communicate with him or her in general, nothing like nothing like make love to me while my husband is upstairs Some thing so delicate needs better communication They animal communication (hunter) is very, very ineffective. May be the source of the animal communication is animal spirit, a derivation of metaphysics or just a new phenomenon from another human theory. Nonetheless it is puzzling, for, continuing that way, we would lost the ability to talk in less than a century.

Now and then I get the impression that the dumb communication is used because it makes sexual activity more appetizing. That way you can make love to a person without wanting to touch the rest of his or her body. No wonder I celibate un-voluntarily for 12 years. If talk is inconvenient in one particular situation, you can still convey the message of love making by a caressing touch. If it is kept going like we will all be dumb. Possibility for big disturbances in a society where 90% of us are disintegrated.

The animal communication is well illustrated by Kesha (attractive, intelligent, nice looking young lady) song which was among the first top songs in that kind of "palmares" recently. The name of the son is Blah, blah, blah. When I used to teach in high School, when everybody started to talk together, to stop them I used to raise my voice and say Blah, blah, blah. I am not sure if they expression is common in the English language, nonetheless Kesha might have read in my space of the psyche, Kesha being young and fresh out of school.

I interpret the song to be saying instead of talking let's get on with it, with the sexual act, although artistically it could be an irony. Let's get on with the sexual part forget the talking part, we are animal, we cannot and should not speak about it. Curiously, in the archetypal psychology description of what should be expected from a mature adult personality is the animal flow of life. I suspect the animal spirit, and animal communication are behind that conception (animal flow), but let's not think about that.

BODY SOUL AND SPIRIT

May be I should start by describing in what sense I am using these concepts. Body is an activity. In it there is the ego and the I. the I is the result of the meeting of the individual soul and the Soul Of the World, as already mentioned above The ego is that empirical sense we have of ourselves, is more related to the past Of course the soul and the spirit are in the body. However we can say also that the body are in them, given that the soul and the spirit are not as substantial as the body and depending on the perspective.

The book called Soul Exposed (starting point from my part of getting human being closer to the Creator) gives a sense of soul in the day to day life situation. Soul is an image; life is a big image. It is more like an artist whereas the spirit is more like a lawyer, associated with science, philosophy and religion. Our creator looks more like the spirit as I saw them both in DP (even in DP we so not really see them but they make their presence felt. The Soul of the World is in us and out of us. There is the Soul of the World structured and the Soul of the World chaos.

Body soul and spirit are what Heidegger called our own most. My DPs make me believe that they are what we have and what brings us the closest to our Creator. In one DP I have seen them all going a different way. Apparently each one of them splits from the body at night and goes its own way. They normally split at night, when soul and spirit play a bigger role in our lives. Still in that DP they where at awe with each other. Later, I have learned that in the present society the sequence body-soul-Spirit are no longer valid, that what stands is body-spirit-soul, meaning that spirit is no longer closer to our waking life, no longer the director of our daily living, the soul is the one playing that role now.

Even with that I wrote the book called Soul Exposed, I decide to keep the spirit as closest to my waking life, and as the director of my life, for soul seems to be a too much bigger deal to take care of one individual at a time. Even our individual soul includes our environment: plant and animals. In my goals there is a foundation. To reinforce it in exercise, I use a hand in which there are coins; the hand is stretched outward. Later in the newspaper they show a potato hand taking from the ground with 5 fingers, it illustrates the environmental aspect of the soul.

The sequence body-soul-spirit stays without neglecting any of the parts.

In the lottery game I played 3 Winnings numbers often, and I reccorded150 times once until I got tired of doing that. In the research on psychokinetic telepathy I chose 3 subject Jennifer

Nadine and Victoria. Recently I had a series of compulsions from conditioning field on body and soul suggesting, so, to let down the spirit from the equation, while my actions s were telling me to keep the sequence of 3 In Hegel and Nietzsche's metaphysics as mentioned above it is question of animal spirit. Now the case seems to be worse that there is tendency to leave the spirit out of the equation entirely.

Saturday it was reported on a show called 16 by 9 on Global TV the case of a pills made out of preservative. They show many individuals who by prescription bought the pills and had trouble with it. The say that the pills have the same effect than morphine and that it is addictive. Looking further it was reported that the company who sold the pills marketed it as an innocent pill like aspirin while the real ingredient in the pill is morphine. According to the report the physicians who were prescribing the pills were lied to. The pill is sold in Canada and in United Sates of America. In Canada it is still being sold.

What I am saying here is it is better to rely on yourself, your body, your soul and your spirit, because it is the way to stay connected with our creator and not get cut in social machination.

Chapter 2

CHOICE OF THE 3 SUBJECTS AND FINDINGS

CHOICE

As subject I have chosen Jennifer Allan, Nadine Chanz and Victoria Spelling.

They are all beautiful, intelligent, attractive women according to me. However, the choice of Jennifer Allan and Nadine Chanz was made more surely because I was receiving Playboy at home, the closest contact I had with women at the time and Tori by watching 90210 and because her picture was available to me.

From the beginning I try to keep it professional, not mixing the research with matrimonial endeavors. Also, not knowing how long it would take to have a result I did not want to ask them to wait for me, to put ourselves in an embarrassing situation. Nevertheless, it seems to be a reason for them not to contact me. I cannot try to get in touch with them myself, which would destroy the purpose of the research, which was to verify somewhat the telepathic concept at first.

The ethical consideration would dictate that HBBs cannot be chosen for research purposes without their consent. Unfortunately or fortunately in this research that is the purpose, to communicate with them without previously contacting them (when it would be possible to ask their consent) in the complete level of life.

It would not be possible for me to choose one individual in each of the 190 countries in the world even if I wanted to, me with my already small budget with no grant from companies or governments. That is why I have chosen only representative of all the world. Nevertheless when we are interested in the Creator we are interested in everybody and everything.

OTHER HBBs WANTING TO PARTICIPATE

All the other 10 women in the tape (will be presented in Findings later) with Jennifer and Nadine wanted to be chosen for the research, it seems, except that I needed only 2 of them.

Later I found that a lot more HBBs would like to participate, including celebrities in Hollywood, politics and in religion. That way I have a number of psychic girlfriends: Amy Avril Britney, Carla (the couple Carla and President Sarcosi are my friends in psyche only, we met in psyche but not in complete life) Christina N, Helena Joanie Ksenia, Lindsay, Queen Elizabeth, all HBBs I never met in complete life level.

While reinforcing my goals on Monday nights, I pick 3 other women. In the goals there are children I want to have. So I think it is a good idea to do the exercise with them in presence of women, psychically speaking. I did not meet them. I saw them in TV. I named one Crash Mom, I saw her in a show with that name. The second ones I call them Maybelline, then I saw Julia's name in a magazine working for the company. Maybe line, Then the other one told me that her name is Genevieve. Another one I named Miami Beach, her picture was taken there. At first I thought it was only 3 but Maybelline told me that they are a group of 2: Genevieve and Julia. They were all my exercise bodies in psyche.

Besides this group of women and the other group Jennifer, Nadine and Victoria, almost all the other women in my psyche are there from their own initiative, there are many.

WORK SESSION WITH THEIR PICTURES AND CONSEQUENCES IN CL

During a telepathic session I work with Jennifer first, then Nadine, then Victoria. She seems to resent that I work with her at last, although I do it that way only because of the alphabetical order of their family names Allan, Chanz and Spelling.

At first I sat down looking at their pictures for about an hour. After many years of doing that, I let down this technique and put them in my Daily declaration instead. Later again I work with them 30 minutes 5 days a week in having psychic conversations with them questioning them plus the daily declaration. I did not use their picture anymore. After a number of years the pictures became old, difficult to handle. Later Nadine told me that Benedict 16 was harassing her. Benedict 16 told me it was because he wanted to make love to her. The picture of Nadine from Playboy magazine I was using was very graphic

There was also Janet Jackson Wardrobe malfunctioning with Justin Timberlake at ball game. I thought Janet was under the influence of a picture of Jennifer I was using with her breasts a bit revealed. There was also the picture of Britney revealing herself, which made a scandal. I thought she was under the influence of the same picture of Nadine I was using and which made the Pope's eyes puffed up. It was may be to avoid causing nuisance for them and others I stopped using their picture while doing the research.

MOVING AND TELEPHONE CUTS AND FRUSTRATIONS FROM 1997 TO 2010

A few years later as I was doing the research on telepathy I decided to add the telephone that is in the telepathic message I send them my telephone number so that they could call me. In 1999 I was asked to move out of the house I was living in 3339 west 42nd. I was sick could not find another place on time, so I lived in a hotel downtown for a month without a telephone with cord in my name. Then the idea to have a cellular telephone came to me. I got one from Fido on a prepaid service deal. The company was just started. I had some trouble with them, discontinued to use there service after a small number of years.

By that time the Fido company became very popular, already gathered a billion $ in asset. I am tempted to believe that using their telephone whereas doing the research on telepathy is the reason why the get rich so quickly.

As was using their phone, one-day I got 500 e-mails at Fido e-mail service and a big number of calls.

After that I had a new telephone number from telus 604 731 4217. I did the telepathic work with it. In September 2009 I had to move out again. I could not continue using the number so I have a new cellular telephone number 604 290 1511. I am still asking them to call me at the cell phone until this book is published if nothing happened with the phone itself. After the publication it will be too late.

The moving around was always mysterious and surprising to me. It may be related to the research, it may not. However for so many years I came to the conclusion that, it is not important to keep the phone number because of the research, that not only it takes few hours for them to know new telephone number, but also they have much more information on my being such as my address, e-mail address and about the events of the past days of my life. I got the idea in 2004, when I came back from New York. In DP I saw all 3 Jennifer, Nadine and Victoria. During the DP they each talked about contact in a different way. Victoria asked me to meet her at her office; Nadine and Jennifer talked about e-mail and letters suggesting that they know my address as well.

Sometime after the beginning of the research in 1997, still now in 2010 as I am writing these lines I feel frustrated asking myself why I do not received a call from them or why they do not contact me any how. Victoria was sending message in the show 90210 to call her. Nadine wanted and may still want to come to live in Canada probably with me. Recently in a psychic conversation with Jennifer, she said squarely if I cannot use her ovule to create the children I can forget about her.

Later it became clear to me that a well designed research would include women, men of all races, age from infancy to adulthood.

In order to cover everybody in the research Jennifer representing all HBB speaking English, Victoria all HBBs of Arabic Descent and me representing all HBBs living on the Equator and the south of it.

FINDINGS

JENNIFER AND NADINE'S TAPE

I chose their pictures in playboy magazines in 1997. In 1998, I bought a video in the store named Virgin on Burrard and Robson, place owned by Arnold Schwasenneger then, Swachennger who is governor of California now. I was spontaneous action, picked the tape without knowing who were in it. It is called Playmate Calendar with Victoria Silvsted on the cover. Almost always one is close to depression, needed to watch these sorts of materials to circumvent the blues.

To my surprise in it there are 12 playmates including Jennifer and Nadine. There are 2 who characterized themselves as an angel: Angel Boris who says that she is not always an angel, that her name is one; and Kelly Monaco who played an angel by wearing white wings. It can be deducted that they compare me with an angel be cause they saw me in their dreams. Lynn Thomas suggested that I should pick her also for the experiment on psychokinetic telepathy. Before I watched the tape I did not see them, I might have seen them on DP without recognizing them. It seems they were all aware of the project in telepathy (Now I realize that the concept angel is what was used in the past and is used in our epoch to indicate the Creator, although it does not seem that anyone is thinking that way except me).

However from all the 12 playmates only Jennifer and Nadine act as if they know that I picked them to do the experiment. Jennifer plays a lot with the red phone in her sequence with a reggae tune playing at the end of it. Nadine says there is man out there, she is thinking of him all the time and showed a German man's headshot. It may be an explanation why she does not contact me now March 30th 2010. It would be a question of nationalism or she thinks that I am German.

During the reinforcing sessions since 1997, we are always in direct communication. I asked Jennifer if she knows my telephone number. Her answer was 604. 604 is the regional code of the telephone number I had. There is the belief in psychology that feelings are more transmissible then data, then numbers. I do not have that conviction, for after the million direct communications I have with many different human beings I am rather convinced that the nature of the message is not a variable.

Saturday night (Today is April 5, 2010) I had in a DP 660 7225 ad to it the regional code 604 and called. There was a certain Chantal at the answering machine with a new number to connect to her 604 664 7858. She apparently moved to a new place. I have never met her or heard of her before to my knowledge. I am going to call her tomorrow to see if I can discover more on her. The point is it is not very difficult to transmit numerical message to someone via direct perception, either direct communication (you will fins out later)

I do not know now if they are playing the snob with me by not contacting me. I do not know if it is because we are of a different chrono age, if the fact that we are of dissimilar race matters. I was in contact with Lisa Dergan when it seemed to me that she was getting close to Jennifer. I lost contact with Lisa and do not know the rest of the story. I have never seen neither Jennifer neither Nadine except in the tape during the research. They may be married or in relationships that prevent them from getting in touch with me. If you do not know what the research is about you may think that I am after them for relationships. After all they may simply not know my contacts for one reason or another.

VICTORIA SPELLING'S BOOK

In it she describes how she divorced her first husband and Married Mac Dermott. She was having some strange moments and strange vibes about a Haitian (I was born in Haiti too) Voodoo Priest before she was about to come to Canada to play in a film. At the end her friends suggested to go and see the woman priest for a psychic reading. After seeing the voodoo priest she came to Toronto to play in the film she said was written by an unknown writer (She was may be referring to the Unknown Reality a book I read around the year 2000 written by Jane Roberts). Mac Dermott was playing in the film too. That's how and where they met. They got married soon afterward.

Mac Dermott is the name of a garage facing a branch of Vancouver Public Library I went to do research this branch of the Library often from 1992 to 2009, because I was living in the area.

Victoria was married to another man divorced him to marry Mac Dermott. Mac Dermott was married to Mary Jo, divorced her to marry Victoria. I have a niece Marie Georgie Prince, living in New York. We call her Marie Geo same pronunciation that the one above. In other words Victoria's Marriage was made by the research in telepathy. When I was reinforcing the project in each session once I use to say to all 3 I "wish you the best". It is clear now my wish materializes itself, for Victoria seems to be very happy in her marriage.

Why did not she contact me? What I said in trying to answer that question about Jennifer and Nadine goes for Victoria too. In her case I know she is married and that could be a problem. In the 90210 one of her friend was sending the message for me to just take the telephone to call her

I never met Victoria; we never communicate except via direct communication and perception. In fact had some feeling for Portia De Rosi. When I knew she was friend with Tori. I discontinued thinking of her in order not to create suspicion about the result of the research. I had feelings for Geri Haliwell. It is reported in a Newspaper her saying I need a Canadian Man (I am Canadian) to fertilize my eggs. When she came to Whistler, I was sick could not try to meet her. Afterward I learned that her and Victoria are two good friends. I did not pursue her further because of that.

Actually I could be with Tori's friends without talking to them about Tori. I judged that that too could raise suspicion on that my mingling with her is purely telepathic, is purely via direct communication.

She wrote a column in Playboy, which was about the research. She played with a red telephone in film that too was about the research. In Scary Movie 11, she played with a play phone with which children used to play before the discovery of the telephone.

Another fact relevant to the research is that around year1999 or year 2000, Victorian came in Vancouver In the hope that I could meet her may be. I think she was staying in a hotel on Burrard Street not very far from where I was living, I remember that they were saying in the radio she was had abdomen pain. If it was now in year 2010, I would meet her and never talk to her about the research. I was a bit slow at that time to catch up with all the events in my life.

Chapter 3

<u>FINDINGS-A</u>

THE <u>TRANSCENDENTAL BEHAVIORS</u> OR DIRECT: COMMUNICATION EXPERIENCE PERCEPTION

I call them transcendental behaviors to simplify I discovered them at the same time as I was doing the experimentation in telepathy Transcendental behaviors are a kind of collective awareness, a bit opposite to collective unconscious of Jung. Sometimes I am tempted to say that Freud discovers the unconscious, Jung discovered the archetypes, and I discovered the transcendental Behaviors.

Nonetheless, Freud, Jung and Adler psychology are very egotistical, of a dictator style, according to me, the way I can explain the anger they had toward each other about psychology at that time. Otherwise, they would all agree to disagree with each other, and at the same time that everyone has the right to have his or her own ideas. The long-standing hatred they had against each other is the sign that they thought there was something wrong with their own ideas. That confirms once more my idea of their egotistical and dictatorial psychology. They did great in their human knowledge quest; there is still a long road to go through. But oh boy . . . . ! Let's go back to our ship.

Freud would say that the TBs happen in the unconscious, Jung would say they occur in the collective unconscious, I say they take place in the Reality field.

Why Transcendental Behaviors were not discovered Long time ago?

Transcendental behaviors are a bit similar to transpersonal psychology, or spiritual work intended not only to heal personal trauma, but also to help HBBs to realize their full potentials. These psychologists have never heard of transcendental behaviours because I have just came up with the idea while doing the research on psychokinetic telepathy with Jennifer, Nadine and Victoria. Some psychologists would object to call anything spiritual a behavior, some others would refuse to mix behavior and spirituality. Although my discovery does not from out of the wind. It was in the field but covered with psychological dust, so to speak. Any way the aim of transpersonal psychology and my psychology are similar: healing and developing human potential to the fullest.

The person I "know" who came the closest to the transcendental behaviors is Alvin Mahrer, because in his book Experiencing, he takes a step back from the way the phenomenon was viewed in the psychology field before that. Before him the person who admitted that he heard voice in her head was considered suffering sever psychological disorder, was put under surveillance in a psychiatric ward. About 80% of psychologists and therapists are still seeing the phenomenon the same way and treating those supposedly crazy persons the same way. However Mr. Mahrer says that they are not as crazy as it would let you believe, that theses persons are communicating with real bodies far away from them, it is really a person to person connection.

And the engine of the connection is liking or some kind of strong emotion between two or more individuals. I am in TBs with the women I mentioned above because we like each other. I am not in TBs with many men because of the question of homosexuality, because of subtle sexual harassment by men I live close by. In Archetypal psychology, it is said that psychic consciousness brings with it erotic consciousness and vice versa (like the transference love in therapeutic treatment is rather a question of awareness). So when it happens between me and a woman I do not notice it much, between a man and me I notice because of my heterosexual option. According to that the erotic awareness calls for psychic awareness and vice versa, the men is not really conscious of what is occurring between them and me. I have in any case a big bunch of men in my space of the psyche, because I am trying to solve problem related to them.

That sort of thinking was the main block to the discovering of the transcendental behaviors where those voices are considered real voices coming from living HBBs near or far, rarely from a dead person. The talkers may be living far or near the person who is hearing his or her voice, but it is like having a space in the listener's psyche, so the communicators are like inside the mind of the listeners. I hear often HBBs committing big crime saying that while pleading their cases that it is the voice in their mind that asked them to commit the criminal action. It is true (Justice may have to recalibrate their thinking to take into account the transcendental behaviors. The voice may be coming from someone looking for revenge, or from a criminal mind, simply from another person who does not like the person in court.

DIRECT COMMUNICATION

We can have direct communication in complete life and in incomplete life. In complete life it takes a physical device, a telephone, Internet, etc. In the incomplete life the communication is done without a device. The communication via the body's cell or the spirit, person to person, so time and space are not a factor. The two persons or beings in communication can be very near each other as the person in the other room, the person sitting next to you in the bus or very far from each other as one in Hollywood and the other in Vancouver living in a basement, Canada, one in South Africa, the other in Alaska. One may be on earth and the other in weightlessness.

This kind of communication is probably faster than the telephone or at least as fast as it is. When I am talking in the telephone some HBBs from afar are communicating with me at the same time via direct communication

After I started doing reinforcing exercises with Jennifer, Nadine and Victoria in psychokinetic telepathy. There were other women who wanted to participate in the experiment, among them, above all Queen Elizabeth, made me realized that it is not because I was fantasizing about these women, that they are the ones who were trying to communicate with me in order to participate in the project. Because I would not fantasize about the Queen, given her prestige and my low social status in a certain way. You know what, these women help me discover direct communication. Before this kind of event was attributable only to the "crazy ones". Britney was called like that too. No, it is rather a manifestation the phenomena called direct communication, direct experience and direct perception that was moving her in a way that could be regarded as erratic.

In other words, the voices we are hearing in our psyche are real voices of real persons whether we know that person or not. Not knowing the person and being not able to recognize his or her voice, may be the reason why in psychiatry the patient having that kind of experience is often diagnosed as having severe psychosis. They are hearing voices . . . Yes they are hearing voices, still voices of real HBB's in the distance or close by, parents friends admirers.

When Jennifer talks to me I recognize her voice. The same goes for Nadine, Victoria' Amy, Britney, Lindsay, Queen E (More details in the book named Kickitwell Or Else). King of Spain and so on. True the person may be dead, but he will tell who he is. That what I discover while doing the research on psychokinetic telepathy.

We do have direct communication in DP also. Haaaaa! In DP the direct communication has different aspects. It may be mind to mind communication, 5 senses communication, feelings communication.

Yet direct communication may be a prolongation or explanation of DP. That DP was published in site www.psychicfacultyandresearch.com

I had a group of HBBs in that DP. They only one I really recognized was the Russian Tennis player: Ana Kornikova. I asked her for an encounter with her she said that she was living too far from me. I did not know at that time that she was friend with any body. I realized there were other HBBs in the room during the DP that I did not quite know, although I knew they were Swedish. In the morning in a direct communication Putin talked to me about Caradeux the name of a big plantation of sugar cane in Haiti. Then I realized that he was in the DP the night before. When I became conscious in another DP I found the woman on top of me nude. The following day she called to say to me that she was an American lender, that she can help me buying a house in USA. At that time I was looking to buy one In Canada. With Putin it was direct perception at night to direct communication during the day, in this one it was DP to complete life situation.

DIRECT EXPERIENCES

It is a dirEct experience, because it does not happen in complete life. While doing reinforcing exercise with Jennifer Nadine and Victoria I saw Victoria wearing a big hat (In Psychology it is called visioning, seeing someone or something from afar). As if she was on a beach. It was not a direct experience; because I was not interacting with her as such, She was miles away from where I was. While doing the exercise I had a vision of her. It was not a DP either, because I was awake, working, and she was probably awake also. At best it was a direct communication. I think it was a direct communication, because I was only trying to communicate with her.

Direct experience is really done during DP. As said above what can be done at that time is almost limitless. It is not just trying to diffuse love energy in complete life when we do not have love outlet. It is not just making love with the most beautiful women who would probably not even see us in CL. It is not just having access to dignitaries anywhere in the world. It is all that and more. The woman makes love with me while pregnant. The woman makes love with me after she has just give birth to a baby, probably because husband refuse to make love with her so soon after the birth of their child. It is said that it is un-proper to make love physically soon after giving birth. So we have direct experiences when they are not so possible in complete life.

In that that kind of experience we can stop wars liberate nations as I did with the Berlin's wall and the Soviet Unions. For details, please see Soul Exposed. I was surprised to learn that war can be stopped by love, not the kind of abstract love, but love between men and women and making love. I have Raya a Russian lady, Angelika a German lady both living in Winnipeg at the beginning of the eighties to corroborate the truth. In DP and direct experiences as suggested above, we are almost like the gods.

Direct experiences are one of the reasons why DP is not like dream during which we are passively receiving the experience. In DP we are actively making our direct experience according to our needs. In direct experiences we can be even with our enemy even though not happily.

Body, soul and spirit may be involved in direct communication, in direct experiences and in direct perception together or each separately.

DIRECT PERCEPTION

At first I knEw I did want to observe myself by recording my dream, not recognized as such in part of the scientific world, dream that some HBBs equate to active imagination or even dark imagination or nightmares. They say "you can dream about it", meaning "you are not going to have it". In the saying there is a bit of metaphysics nothingness, which is equivalent to zip, nothing, negative the absence of everything.

That and all sorts of negative connotations that go with the concept dream that could get in the way, I decided to call them direct perception. Later I discovered that direct perception are not quite the same as dream, because of the study way with which I am having them and because they are tightly linked to the events of my day to day living and that they are rather reality in the incomplete life. Soul Exposed is good example that statement.

Naturally direct perception is what makes human being looks as god, a phenomenon that brings us closest to our Creator, wizardry, in DP everything is possible for human beings. You can meet the queen make love to her, be friendly with her. You can meet practically any other woman and have the same kind of experiences with her. The slightest liking from you to them and or from them to you makes it possible. That is how I met stars like Britney, Lindsay, Avril and a big number of other women and men (in DP of course I never met them in complete life, something I wish I could do), rich and famous, young and intelligent compare to me with a long chronological age and poor hitherto and rather close to the beast, like in Beauty and the Beast. In direct perception we are like flying in the wing of our Creator.

Today (April 7, 2010) at the bus stop on 29 Avenue near Oak I saw a billboard for a film, which is going to open at the end of the month, called Nightmares. Then in smaller letters it is written He knows where you sleep. For a moment I thought it was about me, or somehow the film writer knew that I was going to write this book at this time. Nevertheless, the film illustrates a bit what is said above that instead of dream I use rather the concept DP because of all sorts of not so positive connotations associated with dream including nightmares.

We have the so called nightmare to warn us of what we doing wrongly in our lives and suggestion on how to do it better How much wrongly we are thinking about somebody or something, etc. I suppose that the big hiccup in it is that we do not think of ourselves enough, our body our soul and our spirit we do not observe the Creator enough. We are always running after the external world. That could be a good thing itself if married with running after ourselves. According to me nightmares are telling us to come back to ourselves a bit and hopefully we would ask the question worthiness, that is to say, questioning our creator. I used to have nightmare before, Since I started recording my DP. I do not have them anymore. I do have DPs on bad events about to occur; still I almost always am able to put them in proper perspective. "Nightmare" is a wake up call.

And then we realized also that events like earthquake, tornadoes, tsunamis, human beings who passed away like Hitler, Stalin and other similar big events are also a wake up call. I am not going to develop on that much, but it seems by them Reality is telling us something is wrong and that we could do better.

The DPs we have are about our lives. You can verify that for yourself in the Soul Exposed. In other words our will, desires are the content of our DPs, although our will and our desires are not always obvious to us. We may be also not rational about them. In other words deep down we are free to be, if society does not take the freedom away from us, Some of us are till looking for the lost paradise which is a capital sin. The question was asked to two writers in a show called "Tout le Monde en Parle" (Everybody talks about it) in the French part of Radio Canada last Sunday "Why they writers do always go the past to write?" I do not remember the answer. I thought that they go to the past looking for the lost paradise. In complete life when we do that, we let ourselves open to all sorts bugs including not directing our lives, direction taken by society, wife or husband, sister or brother, peers, friends, community groups, church, governments etc.

We can have DP organized by our body, our soul and our spirit, each separately or all together. Whey they arrange the DP jointly, most of the time we do not remember it.

COMPLETE AND INCOMPLETE LIFE (CL AND IL)

There are what I name complete life versus incomplete life

The person talks to me via the telephone. We are in complete life. The person talks to me via DP, via direct communication, we are in incomplete life. Instead of incomplete life we could say infinite life or relative life. Instead of complete life we could say finite or total life. I prefer to keep the two concepts complete and incomplete life. I do not want to fall back in the metaphysical theory with a totality meaning the absolute form where there is no place for anyone or anybody to grow. Furthermore, I think everything else and human being can change, that is why you see in the vocabulary HBB (I use it a lot) for human being becoming, doe not sound well in English. It does sound very well in French "être humain en devenir" I will have to test it with Native English speaking to find out if Hunan being and becoming(HBAB) sounds better. They say that HBB sounds better

It is said also that the alchemist should have intimate knowledge of metal by blending his soul with it. I visited my brother for 8 days in New York. During one of these nights I had a DP in which I saw myself carrying something very heavy. Afterward, I heard "Metal". This DP is very alike what is said in the book about alchemist

I do not use the infinite and infinite concepts, because they will not satisfy the fact that I can talk to someone living far away in direct communication and I would not be able to say that the person is in infinite life, without appearing bizarre (Infinite make us think of something very distant and not alive), but if I say the person is in incomplete life it will sounds better. So there is a need to use the concepts complete and incomplete life instead of finite and infinite life.

At the time the concept "complete and incomplete life" came to me between 10 and 4 years ago, I did not know much about alchemy, Hermeticism. For me alchemy was the talk about HBBs not so well in their mind and who think they could change any metal in gold. However after reading Hidden Wisdom and the recent DP on the Creator, I changed my mind on it. In Hermeticism "the inanimate world too is endowed with life". It makes sense for this group of HBBs to think like that given that they are chemists where an H an atom of hydrogen mixed with 2 atoms of oxygen give us water. Consequently we can say that the atoms have some kind of life even if they are inanimate. Then my concept of incomplete life means that we are out of the wood this time, given that the Hermeticists talk about inanimate object with life. At the essence of these objects there are knowledge very similar to the DP when I saw what I thought was the Creator.

The difference between complete and incomplete life is not clear at first glance. For we could easily associate the incomplete life with the spiritual life and the complete life with the material life. The problem with those associations is that a person in incomplete life is also material being, the same person in complete life is also spiritual, the same as tings in complete are material being, spiritual at cellular level. Like I said above a bit complicated. The only sure and simple way to differentiate incomplete and complete life is to think that animal, human beings in incomplete life are beyond time and space, while things in complete life they are within time and space.

The concept incomplete life and complete life take us away from the forever debate with materialist group in one side and the spiritualist group on the other side. That kind of debate becomes so pejorative, so divisive and so passé. Any way the transcendental behaviors take place only in the incomplete life.

This way the concept incomplete life, beyond time and space seems to be much more appealing than complete life, limited, within time and space. Being in the incomplete life is being like a god, close the Creator. It is like being in an eternal paradise. Nonetheless, we human beings do better by liking both being on the incomplete life as well as being in the complete life. Wanting too much being in the incomplete life is like wanting too much being in "lala" land, like wanting too much to die.

Lelio my late brother and me were talking together for a whole night after not seeing each other for years. During this long conversation he told me that one time he had lost consciousness in a hospital in Haiti. It was like bragging about how well he felt in the state of unconsciousness that I felt obliged to tell him to stop being happy about unconsciousness in dry tone. Months later he was dead.

I have so many girlfriends in psyche or in the incomplete life. It seems that they like to be there so much that there they are unconcerned about to make the other step to meet me in the consciously. And this state of affairs has nothing to do with any material consideration; some of them are very rich already at a young chronological age. I am thinking of Britney, Lindsay, Carla, Queen E. Avril and some others in other places of the world. The state is so only because of the intrinsic nature of the incomplete life, like said above, almost like being in eternal paradise. So are relationships in the incomplete life is not growing, given that it seems there is no intension to take to the complete level. Now it is lke Zombie relationships. That is why I say it is much better to like the incomplete life as well as the complete life. The spiritual without the material is nothing and vice versa.

In the DP the image I saw with I called the creator, there was a golden color to it. Then in many other DPs, I saw the sky very dark although there are some stars and other bodies. Then after the part where it says that the "inanimate object is endowed with life" the description continuous by saying that it is the alchemist task to propagate this life. Elsewhere it is question of consciousness enclosed in the darkness of matter. The DP above suggests that too.

The author wrote in his book these words of St Augustine I think "For the darkness is lamentable in that the possibilities are hidden from me, my mind questioning itself upon his own towers feels that it cannot trust its own report".

Few days before Italien left Haiti, in a DP I saw near the shore about 3 ladies swimming in the sea. When they saw me out of breath the yelled the Italien's name. In the morning While I was trying to understand the DPs had the previous night, I received a call from Italien (one my brothers) from Haiti. I talked with him, my sister Monise, her daughter Kathia and Kathia's husband, her twin daughters Navidala and Navidalène. Before we close the phone line, I told Italien that I would talk to him again in New York where he is living now.

The DP at night and the call in the morning made the link between the incomplete and the complete life. At night we were in the DP and in the incomplete life. In the morning after the call we were in complete life. That DP was a kind of prediction, a kind of clairvoyance. During that day I did not have a hint that there was going to be a 7 Richter scale earthquake in that country or it was an oversight.

I had another DP in which I saw a huge being in the sea. Myself I was on the beach. At first I thought it was an alligator, then I concluded that it was a big fish. One or two days later I learned that A big fish had killed his keeper in United States of America in an aquarium. The connection is done here again between the complete life event and the incomplete life event. Probably for-seeing what was going to happen in the Mexican Gulf also?

I remember these DPs and these life events well because they are unusual and scary.

Obviously DP happens in the incomplete life (Our Creator is in the incomplete life, may be, but conceiving it the incomplete life is rational). If we say complete life is physical life almost everyone would agree with us. However if we say if we incomplete life is physical life we would raise many eyebrows. Still there are some physical aspects in DP.

First of all, according to research on sleep, there are some physical activities going on when there is rapid eye movement (REM) or synchronize eye movement. The heartbeats faster, the brain's heat elevates. Those are physical activities. Men have penile erection. This last activity is what makes me conclude the eyes start moving in synchronization when we are having a DP for the erection signals the presence of a woman we like or simply a person flashing his or her sexual parts of her body to us. As suggested above there can be a lot of sexual activities during DP, given that at that time we are more relaxed, what erase our sexual barriers and hangs-up.

And can DP cause heart attack? In the history of fatalities there is no case, in which is reported that someone died because he was having dream. It should be the opposite situation; dream heals, makes us sleep better digests and eliminates in a better fashion. A few times I had heart palpitation, I took a few pills (Novo-methacin) for it, the heart came to its regular bit ratio per minute. The heart irregular bit seems to have been another expression of multiple sclerosis and or love trouble.

Second, my own experiences with DP suggest the physical aspect of DP or at least a very thin barrier between the complete and the incomplete life. In that DP I was about to meet a woman when I saw Daniel following me because I was supposed the lover of his wife Maria), he was going to hit me with a soccer punch in the DP, I sat down abruptly and avoid the punch, I woke up with a nose bleed that last many minutes. So the DP which is in the incomplete level of life and the nose bleed which in the complete level of live are very tightly linked and the nose bleed signals a rupture of tiny tube in the nose

Third creation, which happens during DP, is a physical event at the essence.

Fourth we can do almost anything we do in complete life in DP as well. We can hear, see, smell, taste and talk. We can be involved in an accident and looking or reporting it too, we cannot do that one in complete life. It is to say that in Dips the possibilities are endless. However they happen in the incomplete level of life which is different from the complete level of life. For example we could not get a woman pregnant in DP.

After all, direct perception is not really my discovery, Freud and Young record a big quantity of theirs. HBBs are having them everyday, even if they are not always aware of that.

Complete life experiences are easier to extent the transcendental behaviors, that is, it is easier to forget HBBs meet in the complete life than HBBS with whom we have direct communication, direct experiences communication and direct perception. Because in complete life we only have to ignore the person by eliminating all contact with him or her what we cannot do that easily with the TBs. For example, after a problem with Debbie in 1991, I cut all contact with her, however she is still in my psyche, probably dictating to me to talk about her in this book.

We have already seen that DP and direct experiences are basically done in incomplete life. It is not the same for direct communication. They are made rather in complete life and by that I do not mean that the communicators are in sleep state, the communicators are in awaken state very far from each other or seating side by side bodies touching each other, but without speaking to each other making any physical sign, Some of us are very unconscious of a lot of things, we walk as if we are sleeping, like zombies, still this is not a direct communication, nor direct experiences, nor direct perception.

Here is the sentence I like to quote from Jane Roberts and her book The Unknown Reality: "Life bursts apart in all direction as consciousness does". Life is associated with consciousness in her statement. She probably has a dosage of metaphysics in her as any one who has been to school does. With the incomplete, complete life concept, life is clearly associated with the conscious and the unconscious. In her concept reality may be associated with life or with the lifeless, according to scientific practices reality is more likely to be associated with the lifeless. In the incomplete/complete life concept reality is alive but may be not whole.

FICTION AND TBS

Fiction is the biggest block preventing the transcendental behaviors to come to life before the research in psychokinetic telepathy. As said else where in this book there was a negative stigma on the spiritual part of psychology and of life, probably because of the exclusive spiritualism, obviously an exaggeration of things, the negative stigma on the spiritual part was also due to too big preoccupation by science. So this group or part of it was called the mentalist, a word that conveys a very negative connotation. Like above this group of spiritual students and teachers were considered as being crazy. When we say to someone, even today. That he or she is mental, it means exactly that he or she is crazy. We use fiction in a similar manner. To say that something is a fiction is to say that it does not exist, an invention of black imagination. This sense of fiction is very negative in regard to the TBs also despite that they have similar characteristics and because they have similar characteristics. Fiction and TBs are both not see-able, not visible, not touchable, not taste-able, not "odor-able" not "hear-able" for someone in complete life situation. The person sitting beside someone else who is seeing something or some body, let say in a direct communication, cannot hear what is said in the other's direct communication, cannot see the thing or the person in the direct communication, cannot touch them, cannot smell them. The direct communication is close to fiction but is as real as rock. Fiction sharing features with the transcendental behaviors although at the same time being completely different has prevented the latter to be discovered earlier.

My distance with this psychology and certain religions is based on the following thinking: if all these types of psychologies and religions were doing a good work, we would not have the world on the brink of disappearance. HBBs like myself would not be content in using about 2% of our potentials instead of using 90% of them. There is something missing, this missing

Is the getting away from the Creator, which is getting away from ourselves at the end of the line? The getting away from the Creator is becoming more and more pure materialist and less and less ourselves.

LANGUAGE USED IN TRANSCENDENTAL BEHAVIORS

Is something like in another world, can be a group of words non related to each other, two words, one word. I know creole, studied German and Spanish in school, speak and write English and French. So for me, in my direct communications, there is a mixed of these languages without any consideration grammar. In a few sentences there all the languages together. The words have their special meanings or morpheme. For example be-ing for the Creator or Reality is called "bayagn", ambidex= bisexuality (I remember it because Ana Kornikova asked me the question in a DP). Of course once in a while complete grammatical sentences are used.

In the transcendental behaviors everything used to communicate is an image, not restricted to language, is full of pictures and feelings and also the other 4 senses as in hearing, seeing smelling, and tasting and touching (most of my DPs happen the darkness). I suppose that other HBBs communicating with me learn my language as it is described above. And I suppose also that for the learning my languages the other communicator takes only a few days, given in the deep down we know all human languages more or less.

MUSIC AND TBS

It is inspired to me by listening and watching a video on Jazz called Swing the Velocity of Celebration, a film by Ken Burns I am a bit a fan of Jazz because it was played a lot at Radio Canada once. I even want to buy a car, Lamborghini; I saw it in a poster on the sky train billboard while there was a Jazz Festival in Vancouver. So the video is at the end of the continuum, not at first. Watching the video was inspiring in the sense that it is surprising to see how close the Jazzmen and women came to discover themselves the transcendental behaviors.

1939 when the Jazz musical reached its pick in United States was then a quiet year on the surface for HBBs like you and me who a not historian. The history HBBs knew already was that the Second World War was inevitable and that it was going to start the same 1939-year. The Jazzmen and women knew, but they were kind of oblivious to their own knowledge. It seems to me that the Americans were dancing feverishly to the sound the very popular jazz music in 1937 in prevision of and to counter balance what was going to happen to the world with the war that was about to be declared. Just before the war the Jazzmen and women tried to transfer the fever to Europe, but Hitler would not let them pass through, denigrate them and sent them back to America. My theory is that knowingly or unknowingly the jazzmen were trying to stop the second world ward.

However, my interest in the jazz is more in the conception that was behind it. They called it Body and Soul Music, although one important element of this equation is missing, it is the spirit. They said that that the jazz bit was beyond time and space, the same exact definition I gave to the transcendental behaviors although I did not know about the connection with jazz before I watched the video last week (Today is August 3, 2010). It is that way I say that viewing the show was inspiring. For beyond time and space summarizes a field in which can be placed also the Creator.

I do not know much about jazz musicians, May be they were starving, in debauchery or may be they are like you and me, I do not know their story. Ella Fritz Gerald and Billy Holiday were brought up in poor situation in the segregated, male oriented America on their time. That is all I know about them.

Symbolism and Metaphors

I could say 95 % of, direct communication, direct experience and direct perception' content is in symbols or metaphors. The use of symbols is probably for a reason of the economy of space. In other words we can say more in symbols than in written words. I suspect also many used symbols trying to hide their ideas as they do in spy agencies. This enterprise seems to be a waste of energy. For Amanda was one of my tenants and I used to symbolize one millions $ by a bag of sugar. Many times when she arrives home and I am in the kitchen, she come there, pull a plastic bag from under the sink and plays with it, meaning she knows something about the million $ symbolization. As I did not talk to her about it, I do not know how much she knew about it; at least she was aware that it is something important.

When Heidi first came to live in this house on 20th Avenue Vancouver BC, one of the first things she talked to me about was that she needs a bicycle. In my goals there is that after I buy a car I need to buy two mountain bikes and a house bicycle. So she knows about me, my goals before coming to live in the house, that is via the transcendental behaviors. This one is not a pure issue of symbolism. Nonetheless it reinforces the problem that is to say there is no where to hide, some HBBs will know you and thing about you without or before physical contact.

The use of symbol also simplify things for us, instead of representing 100 objects or pictures by themselves we use one and two zéros. It is simpler that way. Actually the use of symbol is in this sense not only a simplifier, but also memory help. If you have 10 words to remember, let say sandwich, healthy, work, counseling, meditation, telephone, dream, gateau, femme, bon, it will be easier to remember if you pick the first ten letters: s h w c m t d g f b, even better if agglomerated in shwcmtdgfb.

It is still surprising to me that we can retain the 10 words in an easier fashion when we reduce the used space, for memory being not substantial the used space should not matter.

There is what we call tricksters in psychology. They are like a psychological trap; no matter the measures you take you do a bad thing involuntarily. One of the causes of the stricter is being too literal. So metaphors are a good way to avoid those psychological traps.

I notice also the one who communicates the most transcendentally with me, Britney is called: "flute-à-bec", speaks French and creole. Go and talk to her about that, she may be totally oblivious to it.

After making love with Lindsay, I was happy, thinking that she was happy too. Then in another DP the same night I saw myself behind the steering wheel a van looking outside. I saw Lindsay wearing a very sexy skirt in front of the van on ground. She talks to me in kind of sign language telling me 'm' couche avec ou (I made love with you) but you are not my boyfriend. Then she showed me a man saying "he is my boyfriend"

I felt attracted by her more during the talk in front of the van, probably because of the skirt she was wearing and because of they word "we made love together". So she speaks creole too. However that makes another important point in my idea of applied philosophy or psychology in general. The point is that—as said Arthur P. Ciaranicoli, PH D" and Katherine K. in the Power of love—"After a great moment, particularly in sexual moment lovers reassert separated-ness . . . after sadness of distancing . . . . Threat of autonomy may give an impulse to flee the relationships altogether or enter into another affair to preserve identity, separate from the beloved".

In other words after that great moment or highest form of experiencing with Lindsay, afraid of loosing her identity and autonomy, she denied the experience. This psychological point is important, because I suspect it is behind of a great quantity of infidelities, separations and divorces so common in Hollywood and in society at large (Relation Amoureuse) a fear that will not last long if we can resist the few moments of it.

That illustrates also that love in complete and incomplete life are very similar.

Still the transcendental behaviors especially DP is not to be confused with complete life situation. The person you see in your DPs may be a complete different person in complete life situation (some of the women appeared sometimes as a man). The person can be totally alien with her deeper part or for some reason or another not totally connected to it. I have 2 examples of that: first is about Oprah, in a DP I saw he she talked to me about a work I was doing that I called cognitive re-labeling and suggested that she would give me money. I wrote her a letter and told her of our psychic encounter. I do not have any answer of that letter.

Same as for Denzel Washington, in the DP he was sitting behind a long table in a mall. He offered me some money that I refused. He said to me I want to give you money, you refuse in a theatrical way. I wrote him a letter in which I asked him to send me the money he offered in the DP. I have no answer of this letter either. At last. After months, the letter came back to me; Mr. Washington may have not received it.

The situation in DP can be the opposite of what it is in complete life, for all sorts of reasons. One reason is the use of metaphor. It is very frequent during DP. For example despite the clear words of Mr. Denzel Washington "I want to give you money, you refuse", what he may mean is to go in a mall rent a space to put a long table to sell my books, as I had started to do once. So this reason can be summarized in this, the plurality of meaning of one DP.

The symbol of my self is a circle with a small sun inside of it, something I pick spontaneously. Apparently we need a geometrical figure in those kinds of symbolism. One very good reason to have symbolism not mentioned above is it makes it easier to know what is in our imaginative space at a given time. If I see a sun in a circle I know it is myself. If I see a bull I know it is my will (The bull in a stampede in Calgary, beginning of July 2010, recently killed a young man, it may not be pure sport after all). Symbolism very important indeed, it allows us to see the "unseeable" a solid tool in spiritual development.

According to archetypal psychology "All realities are primarily symbolic or metaphorical". The scientific HBBs say that the entire material world was packed in on atom. Those two explanations of existence are not too far apart after all. Except I do not see the observation of the creator in order to ground its truth in any of them.

Chapter 4

TRANSCENDENTAL BEHAVIORS
AND OTHER TOPICS

"LE MAL DE L'ART"

It is an allusion to Artist as Marilyn Monroe, Elvis Presley, Michael Jackson, and Emile Neligan who died while they where on top of their artistry and younger ones as Lindsay, Britney, Mel, You have suicidal behavior. It is what I call "le mal de l'art" for in their work they are dealing with metaphor a psychological phenomenon that attract such behavior. According to Archetypal Psychology and Hillman 1964, Ziegler 1980, Soul metaphorical nature has a suicidal necessity, a "morbidism", a destiny different from the world claim and that the sense of weakness, inferiority, mortification, masochism and failure is inherent to metaphor (embraces the shadow of things) which defeats consciousness understanding as control over phenomena. So the artists above and many others or even all artists in one way or another are victim of "le mal de l'art"(translated more or less: art sickness). I think in that sense, the artists playing a role in the so called reality TVs, movies, would not be victimized by this metaphor phenomenon, not using metaphor a lot, although I cannot tell really, not knowing those artists. Furthermore, the role they play in these films are something ephemeral, no time to be victim of metaphor, even if they were using metaphor. From now on the phenomenon would be considered in a treatment conceived to cure Artist.

Does the same phenomenon affect HBBs in the society at large, meaning Hobbs who are not artist? I am thinking of Princess Diana's sudden and untimely death. Was she a victim of the morbid necessity inherent in metaphors? Although she was not an artist as such, or not a declared

31

artist, her death looks similar to the artist misery. Is the phenomenon another facet of the decline in the Western culture, a lack of imagination? All questions I have no answer for.

Nonetheless, we do not need to have university degree to understand that metaphor is used by almost everyone in society. Life itself a big metaphor given that soul is fundamental to life, recognizably or un-recognizably. We have our answer. Misery in life is partly caused by the morbid necessity of metaphor used by soul.

In the humanistic theory human misery would simply be explained by disintegration between human potentials.

JUSTICE AND TBS

In the judgment of the case of Alexa a little girl that was hit by a drunk driver and lost her life afterward, the judgment was adequate. Alexa's mother said that justice was served because the driver is sentenced to spend long time in jail and community services". She also demonstrated a sense of hope. The law concerning this kind of event will be rethought and will be call Alexa's Law. However the sentencing will be made in November, the book may have already been published by that time. Without the sentencing I do not really know if I will publish it

Given that transcendental behaviors are pervasive behaviors, it makes it more imperative for the judges to be more themselves while judging each case in other to come up with the right judgment. The lawyer arrived at the hearing for dismissal, red my Writ of Summons the whole time, than ask for the dismissal of the case. The judge accepted. True it was my time to point out the trick to the judge, with the experience as a judge, he was able to see that the lawyer had nothing to say about the case, which where already set up for trial. The transcendental fact in the case is that I already had a wrong dismissal at work previously that I cannot refute because of money to hire a lawyer, at the law society in BC they were furious about me after I started to advance in court with the case by my self with their help. They cut me out.

The lawyer had read these in me transcendentally and was convinced that anything he told the judge was going to get him a dismissal. It was not because the case had no merit but because I had a similar past of dismissal. Via the TBs HBBs (human being and becoming) can read your past that is of interest to them to the second instances. The judges do not have to guess these transcendental readings; they just have to be themselves to make the good judgment.

Before the case went for trial, the other party did not present himself in time. I went in front of another judge and asked for finding the defendant guilty. The judge said the Canadian laws did not allow him to do that. In the morning preceding the hearing the defendant transcendentally told me that he couldn't be there because he was in California. The defendant lives in Minnesota, he went to live to Hollywood for a while to justify his new fame and riches which was instead my fame and riches, what I was trying to settle in the court.

I met the defendant many times in transcendence; he was trying to settle the case for much less than I asked for. In one DP he was in a sort of truck full of dry grass, telling me that way that I do not deserve much for where I was born they only plant sugar cane. This DP and many more were in back ground of the case as I presented in the court.

I hope there will be in the court system a forum to present transcendental event as evidence. Of course it would take also the usual complete life evidence.

LOVE

Transcendental behaviours are relaTed to love. It's like saying the transcendental behaviors are behaviors of love. First they happen in the Reality field which more like what they call astral light, a place where all humans and everything are in elemental form or other reduced form, or in essence and which we could name the field of love, the or the field of Reality. In other part of the book we write that it in intimate action, the TB behaviors are behavior of love in that sense too.

Second, when you start having DPs the persons you will most often see are the persons you like or dislike or love or hate, later it will be HBBs with whom you have a common ground your colleagues, bosses, persons you may meet in the future, etc. Later again you will be able to see almost any one in the world you want to communicate with. in your DPs.

As already mentioned in this book, almost everybody I come in contact with a while after I started the research behave as if I wake up in them the ability to use the transcendental behaviors. The person, the woman I meet in the street, whom I never met before will start a conversation with me normally in TB. She will say I am married or I am not married (or smiles at me in complete life) and so on. And almost always they will say I love you. They never say I like you or you please me, the great majority of them will say I love the first time we meet in the street, in a bus, in a mall via the TBs. It is why I state that the transcendental behaviors are in a field of love, the Reality field. It is may be why also I get sexually harassed by so many men. I wake up in them their ability to use the transcendental behaviors. I was going to say their ability to love There is a close relation between the wake up of eroticism and spirituality, close relation between, direct communication, direct experience, direct perception and love. Because they happen in the field closer to our Creator.

This way I have a number of lovers, prestigious and less prestigious, rich and less rich local and international in psyche.

It said in this book many times this love between human beings is manifested only when an individual or a group can take other human beings in that place within themselves where their divine part resides (not necessarily substantial). That what happened between me and all other HBBs I come in contact with probably. Nonetheless we have to remember that there are about 8 billions HBBs on the planet. What about them, those I do not meet and those who would not listen to a word from me. Their natural loving or divine parts in them are they dormant or buried under excessive materialism, cement and bricks, or lost in the cloud of equally excessive or exclusive spiritualism? In the context of these two extremes of the continuum we are loosing ourselves, getting away from our Creator, Reality. Our natural loving potentials are fading away as well as all the other parts of us. In that there can be mo genuine love around.

Love in transcendental behaviors in the sense that any transcendental behavior is intimate behavior (person to person, person to animal, person to things.

Freud was the first to develop the pleasure principle in psychology and according to his theory on human beings we are almost all about love, although it is to believe that the love he was concerned with is only sexual love. According to some authors, his followers all love are sexual love. With the transcendental behaviors the matter is about sexual love and spiritual love equally. My observations do not allow me to conclude otherwise.

SELF LOVE

It is an important part of life and of psychology. It is more a harmony between the individual and complete and incomplete life environment. Self-love is the result of this kind of harmony. A lot of implications are in there such as disharmonious society create self-hatred, self-hatred creates disharmonious society. Self-love is the love of the Soul of the world, so the love of the world. If self love is felt in the perspective of the incomplete life activities then we are in for a good start, for as written elsewhere above, it appears that I awake the capacity to use to the transcendental behaviors in each individual I come in contact with one way or another, the capacity of self love, and more or less capacity for harmonious life.

Of course there is a relation also between self-love and peace, the reason why I was thinking of "Gylanic" Europe when I started writing about the subject. Because relatedness between self-love and peace means equally relation between war and unloving self. Some body says war is individual hatred-ness multiplied in a million. The only thing I can see here is that we cannot love ourselves while drifting away from the Creator in our thought. In other words drifting away from the Creator means drifting away from love and peace, getting closer to war and event like what is happening in Afghanistan now, like the stand off between North Correa and South Correa and event like Hiroshima, the Holocaust, event like the genocide in Somalia, event like tee two world wars, event like the number of nuclear missiles with atomic bomb aimed the head of all individuals and living thins on the earth, and so forth. Away from the creator in our thinking is quite the same as being away from life.

When we do not have DP one night or think we do not have, the phenomenon can be explained the following ways

1. We had them, but too involved in making them to remember them.
2. There is a psychic shift
3. We had them, still block them by forgetting them
4. We did not have them at; this one is very unlikely situational state

WHAT I LOOK FOR IN MY DPS

I started by looking for a lot of things that seem not relevant to the entire humanity, however the 5 below look like of a universal application

- AppLied philosophy point (parapsychology or psychology)
- preDiction: precognition, clairvoyance, and retro-cognition
- CatHarsis to de-energize where there is too much psychic energy
- Our Goals
- The Senses

Psychology in the sense that not only our DPs are psychology, but also are spiritual psychology, in the sense that they bring us closer our Creator and in direct contact with It once in a while, spiritual psychology as opposed to psychology in laboratory. So we are working in a all that exist field with an acute sense of despair and fear of making mistake, fear of misinterpreting our insights, and courage in regard to the god and goddesses. And somewhat satisfied of trying to lift, to give a booster to humanity.

It seems that there is prediction in each DP. I am not very good at that because I consider that the time to discuss prediction in DP is past long time ego, and because above all, my resentment toward what I call, the misfortune prophets create fear on the gods and the goddesses, the Creator for adhesion, tactic which never seem to be successful, which probably is part of the causality in the forgetfulness in regard to the Creator.

Another element that is almost always present in DP catharsis to make newness acceptable, to appease our psychological and physical hurts, to erase our psychic scarce, to make us ready for spiritual development. I still do not understand why event that we faced a long time ago can affect negatively or positively our present life. According to the behaviorist and that psychological school there is no causal and circular relation between past and present events. Sometimes I have a tendency to think so too, although I may be wrong with that tendency. Materialists can sound a bit too materialistic any way.

Some of my of my goals are described somewhere in this book, they are my (mine because they must be different of yours) particular goals (some compares not having goals as living in nothingness). However it says that goals are important in everyone's life. They constitute the cursor of physical and our psychological life or complete and incomplete life. I realize that as soon as we have one small goal. There is a lot more items that append to it. One big example is my goal to have a unified African country. This has taken me in wild landscape, to the point that I would hesitate to have if I knew in advance its consequences, if I knew that African Union is linked to cold war, that I would have to get rid of that first before the actual African union, if I knew that I would have to establish peace in the while world, fix the problem of hunger in certain parts of the world before I can realized my small goal which the unification of Africa.

I look for the senses (hearing, taste, and so on) in my DPs, basically because I do not want to leave the complete life away I do not want to forget about it despite the belief of the magician that the slightest light can disturb the occult experience. Having DP is having a very deep spiritual experience. After having so many we can lose touch with the complete life reality. It is why it is better I think to look for them in DP.

Furthermore, there is no better tool to sharpen our senses, to keep them alive than DP. When HBBs are in their late chronological time (old age), the tradition is that they are about to loose most of their senses, especially the hearing, and seeing senses. However, according to my researches on psyche, the psychokinetic telepathy this state of affair need not be. By exercising them in DP they can stay as sharp as they were at a younger "chrono" age. Any way if the body' s cells are renewed constantly there is no rational explanation to become old and die.

IMAGINATION

There is the talk Of dark imagination (like the scare with the volcanic smoke in Europe, the gas scare in the Gulf and BP), when we imagine bad things that could happen to us. We could even have active imagination, we could be anything we imagine consciously, according to positive thinking, and the imagination in which we have interest now: passive imagination. They call it also the imaginative "I". That is in DP we have passive imagination.

Most psychologists, magicians or spiritualists thinkers maintain that psychic processes are best done in the darkness. According to Gurdjieff analyzed in the book Hidden Wisdom even the feeble light of consciousness is enough to change completely the character of a psychic process (while it makes many of them all together impossible). It is like a necessity to make these experiences in the darkness.

However, in my case I do not see why it should be like this. It his true that about 85% of my DPs happen in the obscurity (15% with light), still I am not persuaded that it has to be that way. Last night I had a DP that last for a long time. In it something was happening that I could not see in the darkness, but I had one of the best good feelings in my life. May be there was a woman making love to me, A woman that I would see in the previous TV show before I went to sleep. It occur in the darkness for many possible reasons: may be I did not like the physical body of the woman; may be the woman did not want to be seen with me in DP for she has a boyfriend or a husband; may be the woman did not like my physical body; the counting could go endlessly. I cannot think, though, any reason that would make it a necessity to have the DP in the darkness. For the reasons cited above, I would be more worried that who I thought war a woman, was in fact a man, then I would hot be having those kind of experiences in DP (although I an living in the same house than at least 3 homosexuals) because of that, the experience would be repulsive to me, although I agree that human beings have different sexual habits.

At the other extreme in the imaginative continuum, a man told me that he never had a dream. He was about to edit a book for me "Kickitwell Or Else" when he told me that. I think he meant to say that he never has been conscious of his dreams, given that it is impossible for someone not to have dreams. Nonetheless, what he told me is not really a surprise, it is a general and a dangerous issue in the society at large: a lack of imagination. Psychologists think that TV replaces their ability to imagine with TV series and movies, and at the long run eliminate the ability. I do not know if TV is the only culprit of the matter, even though the disappearance of the ability to imagine in the individual will eventually bring him and his society's disappearance as well. Lack of imagination is probably linked to the forgetfulness of the Creator.

The imagination mentioned is not similar to imagination noire when HBBs sit down and imagine a list of bad things that will or will not happened to them. That kind of dark imagining is rather a sign of a lack of imagination, or a lost of the ability to imagine. The imagination is neither a synonym to active imagination that we do when we are awake. The kind of imagination in the paragraph above is similar to thinking while having a DP or having DP is imagining. It is an activity that ensues in the incomplete life, comparable to the activity and capacity of the soul. You can have a-hands-on-practice to be familiarized with the Soul activities in the Soul Exposed written by me. It is not similar to the numerous books written by Simon Freud on dreams, because the Soul Exposed, I show how the images in the incomplete life are coupled with the activities in complete life.

Images is the domain of soul or soul is made of images, source of images are dream image, fantasy image or poetic images, according to me and psychology of archetype although I am in disagreement with archetypal psychologists in many points such as the will, decision and choice" According to archetypal psychology of we must disregard those which makes me ask myself how do I know which foot to put upfront, if I do not have a will, if I cannot choose one? They also promote life in the edge. I live almost all my life doing that an I got nowhere, none of my goals is created and I am not chronologically young. I find that living life on the edge is a misdirection, a reckless one as that. However there are also lot of good points in the psychology of archetype such" we are a in the psyche, the psyche is not in us, we are in the dream, the dream is not in us: imagination becomes a method of comprehending and investigating psychology, sensitivity to traditional continuity, the significance of psychopathology" and so on.

Choice is very, very important for me in life for many reasons. With so many things in front of us, so many HBBs, we cannot deal with all of them in a lifetime, we must make choices. And then choice help us to understand why there are bad things in life, The Creator is perfect. Bad things happen because we have the choice to go with the Creator or not. We choose not to go with the Creator. That is how free we are, we are free not to go with even the one who created us. That is how fundamental freedom and choice are to life.

Instead of making a nice speech on images and dream and soul, the last chapter will be a report of my DP (similar to dream) and how they link with complete life situation.

THE FALL OF THE ROMAN EMPIRE

It is rather a reference to the Occidental culture which, according many thinkers, is on the descending side of the mountain of life. In one recent DP I visited China with a woman, she disappeared, come back later and we continue the visit together. What was peculiar to me in the direct perception during her absence I spent the time going down many steep mountains, some times a bit scared, sometimes not, the experience was so nerve racking, it was like I spent the whole night doing it.

Some of the causes of the Western cultural decline are in Heidegger book Mindfulness. I noted a few

Cultural progress become a goal in itself
Arbitrariness
Disruption of every relation of beings to the truth of be-ing (be-ing can be replaced by the Creator, beings by human beings)
Illusion of cultural modernity of what has already been in the epoch (new version of Iphone)

Technology (space Shuttle)

Negativity of metaphysics

Dis-humanization

In plain terms it comes down to "hush hush." "à la va vite". We are in a rush, running after everything, everybody else except ourselves.

Arbitrariness is to say that we are going no where despite the piles of studies we are conducting in many subjects, despite that we can send a plane to the moon, we are going no where because we do not have an aim. I have heard the question so many times "what is the purpose of life" Do we really need to know the answer of the question. Let say we know the answer, what would be different in regard to the way we are living our lives now. For me the better question would be how can I make my life more authentic, more livable? Instead of always asking those questions, why don't we just shut up and live?

The arbitrariness can be costly. I finished writing the Soul Exposed in 2004; I approach at least a hundred editors. The book is still unpublished, although it is what we need to read the most in our Western world in other to stop going down the mountain of culture and to start to climb up. The book is the revival of imagination, a bit more spirituality, and a bit more soul in our life. Busy running to go nowhere, we lost track on recognizing what is good for us. It is a fundamental part of the cause of the declining of the Western Culture.

You give a space Shuttle I take it, I give you an "Imaginal" Vessel you do not take it. Why?

The cultural decline is not something confined in the Western culture according to me. The DP above is an indication of that. For one thing the success in technology that the westerners have has a big impact on the entire world. Nowadays the decline of the world culture or the decline of culture in the world is a more appropriate concept in the sense that it describes the situation more accurately. The fundamental purpose of this book and the other books I wrote is an attempt to stop the decline and help us in becoming more spiritual.

Of course the DP is alluding to depth psychology, Then why in China? The Eastern HBBs have a different kind of psychology, a different way of understanding the psyche, the soul the spirit and life. We talk about the decline in the culture in the West, not in the East. The underlined part is that the culture in the East is not in decline. I am not very sure of that. During the Olympic game in China picture of Beijing was shown, the air is so polluted, nothing to make us think that everything is going well there. Besides, China is still a communist Country, although there is some effort made there in other to change their economic rules. Communism and materialism exclusive go hand in hand. Pure materialism is not the right context for spiritual development.

Viewed that way westerners may be even better off in terms of spiritual development. The permanent wars in the East is physical sign of that they are not better off there.

They say that in the eastern psychologies the ego is very "relativised" it is a good thing given that the culture of the ego like in monotheism religion plays a big role in the decline of the Western civilization. However being non-egocentric does not necessarily create a spiritualist attitude. Or a platform for the development of spirituality.

The concept depth may be important in psychology; we are not going to be more spiritual just because of that, because we may be still very disintegrated, we may still be at war inside of us. War in the world right now is a sign of that also, a sign of inner turmoil

After all in relation to the DP mentioned above, in archetypal psychology it said that depth and vertical direction, literal physical location are very important are primary metaphor necessary for psychological thinking.

Chapter 5

<u>PROBLEMS as RELATED to the TBs</u>

There is what I discovered and named Lisa Effect: living in a room close to a person with the name Liza may give some psychic access to another person name Lisa who can be very far from you. It is well described in Book with the name "psychokinetic phenomenon". In the case with Lisa it was a pleasant situation.

Here and now it is not. I moved in a third house, this house where I am living just a bit before January 2010. There are 4 other men living in the same house. Some of them suggest homosexual relation. When they recognized that I am not into that kind of thing they take a step back.

Peter is one of them started to harass me since day one and until now. This Morning (Wednesday April 14, 2010) I woke as usual at 7 am. I choose this spot of time to wake up because I noticed that everyone else is still asleep, so the toilet is free to use. Exactly when I am about to go the washroom I heard the door closed, Peter was inside, It is not a crime to want to have sexual relation with someone else. In my case it is big a problem from a man. I had to pee on a towel and washed afterward this morning. The collision in the toilet happened many times. It is not attributable to the phenomenon observed with women living close by and synchronizing their period. In this case here it is sexual harassment through the psychic channels, through the transcendental behaviors, another kind of harassment.

With the ability to make transcendental behaviors we are or can be constantly in communication with almost everyone in the world. In any case it is a possibility. When we are living close by the communication can be even more intense even more intense.

He reminds us also that the "Catholicism" is a male religion and of the bible verse "Peter you are a rock and on it I will built my church" a sexist stamen and propaganda.

CERTIFICATE OF ACCESS TO CHILDREN AND ADOLESCENT

In my case an adult someone else will not try to force himself on me mentally or physically for sexual favors. However if it were a child or an adolescent, they would have no chance to ward off the predator. That is why I think states should have a law preventing adult (coach, teachers, churches) to have access to children and adolescents without a certificate in which sexual preferences are declared. Usually homosexual are cool. They do not try to overpower, at all costs, another person for sex. The bisexual (they practice sexual dictatorship, they do not care for someone else other sexual preference. They only want everyone else to be like them. They are more are more pernicious un regard to that matter, under the cover that they have a wife or husband or girlfriend or boyfriend, it easier for them to abuse children and adolescents. The certificate will be a deterrent, will allow children and adolescents to exercise their rights, to have a sexual option.

PATHOS

Another Problem with the transcendental behaviors is that one can get the sickness of other HBBs unknowingly. I mysteriously end up with the little toe of the right foot hurting. Monday April 12, 2010, I went to the doctor's office (West-End Clinic) for some pills, the person's first name before me in the waiting list is Jennifer. What is more is that she is pronouncedly limping in one foot. Somehow I was in telepathic link with her even though she is not the Jennifer Allan, subject with whom I am making the experiment in psychokinetic telepathy. The fact of the matter is that in the concept telepathy there is pathos Greek word translated by suffering by some. In the beginning of the book I described all sorts of miseries I encountered during the experiment. They are explained by the pathos in telepathy too. Still we are describing problems in transcendental behaviors in which there are also feelings.

Nevertheless, the question is the Jennifer at the doctor's office the one who has caused my mysterious little toe hurt, or is the real source in my being or are we both have not much to do with it, or is Jennifer Allan one of the subjects of the psychokinetic telepathic research related to our pain?

Alan Prince ET Eddy Cantave were both my nephews. They both died inadvertently and young during the time of the experiment in psychokinetic telepathy. It is true that at the time of their death it was a wild place in Haiti where the "macoutes" (secrete police, the word first meaning a shoulder bag made of hard leather worn by middle age HBBs in the country) were all over killing their opponents and taking what they have. It is true that I had a number of DPs on Eddy but they came with Devaise Eddy's father. It is true that almost all Devaise's brothers are dead at the same time. It is true that Devaise's name is closed to mauvaise (French for bad although he is a good person). They are 2 painful events for me and occur while I am doing the experiment in psychokinetic telepathy make me think of pathos. And that there could be a connection between the death of Alan Prince my nephew and Jennifer Allan the subject? I picked her without her consent because the purpose of the research is to demonstrate that we can have details communication with any one anywhere in the world, even those we do not know and who do not know us?

Another case of pathos and the experiment speaks to my nephew Genio Prince who is alive but who was almost dead after receiving a bullet in his behind

The death of Lelio Prince is another event, which causes me pain while I am doing the experiment in psychokinetic telepathy. Who knows what?

There are so many HBBs wanting to communicate with me via the transcendental behaviors, that sometimes it can be a problem of decision and action. I have all sort of compulsions during the writing of this book; now and then I am paralyzed, unable to go ahead to the next paragraph. Next part, or the next chapter. I am solicited by HBBs from all sides in order to talk about them in the book, while I am trying to focus rather on the phenomenon name psychokinetic telepathy.

Pathos also because when the gods come to the human space they are like affected being just because they are not at the godly place, they are also suffering of being away from the Creator, according to what I have learned in Archetypal Psychology.

There is the man who was working for my father they call him Cedieu (for this is god); he was limping on one foot. I have many DPs on a man called "Cedieu" and he is limping on a foot. I am still having foot problem. It is not clear to me yet if the Cedieu, he is may in incomplete life now like my father, in the DPs has something to do with the one in IL, either if the one in the DP are metaphor for real god. I am perplexed on that, however I may have suffered because of that DPs and him and I still not get or understand the clear message of the whole situation.

In "Kabbalah" it is question of "heavenly wrath". "The Lord is a man of War"(Hidden Wisdom, a Guide to Western Inner Traditions, by Richard Smoley and J. Kinney) Is there a link between the past uprising in Thailand, Korea, Turkey, war in Iraq, Afghanistan and the unusual natural disasters, such as the leak of gas in the sea and what is said in the Kabbalah? They may all be connected wit the idea that the Creator is god and a male, despite the ridiculousness of it.

43

Strangely enough yesterday Monday May 31 It was the day when Israel war boat open fires on a civil boat transporting wheel chairs, and other equipments of the kind to the Palestinian via Gaza stripe from Turkey killing 9 un-armed protestors. Israel becomes a new belligerent. I noticed that during the recent war with the Palestinians. Israelites were killing 1000 of Palestinians a day, while the "Hamas" missile was killing may be 1 or 2 Israelites a day. And that lasts for a big number of days. It was like a massacre under our eyes the rest of the world. And then the real reason behind it, I guess. was the election of the American President Barack Obama. In Israel they thought was going to be he was going to be pro-Palestinian. Since his presidency for about a year, it does not give any reason for someone to make any such conclusion. How many civilians Palestinians killed under the banner of this false assumption, thousands and thousands. The victim becomes the aggressor. History repeats itself. We can forgive, how many times?

I would not say what they say in Kabbalah" (may that belief in Kabbalah makes them the warrior they are today. I would say rather, we are using our freedom to forget our Creator more and more and that is the cause of all sort negativities in the world, including violence, famine and natural disasters.

Also the pathos is for keeping our emotions awake. The situation in life right now is set up to kills our emotions, for us to live like zombies, to close the door to our inner potentials (another source of violence). There is work 9 t0 5, boulot metro, dodo, it is said in French. Then, living with the machines is good up to a certain point, they help us to work less, however, on the long run we become like the machines themselves (many times I find myself living on pilot without any consciousness). All that- and other dis-humanizing ingredients—are against everything to stay as a human being with emotions. The pathos helps us in that sense.

It is what is developed in the big religions, especially in the Catholic religion with the cross walk (could also symbolize a creation). Obviously there misery is exaggerated. There are as many reasons for enjoyment in life as well as for feeling the pain. Then their "god" is an egocentric male. I thought any child would understand that the Creator couldn't be a male or a female or even a thing, given that it created them all (I can create a pencil, can I become a pencil? No way). He can appear as a male, as a female, as a thing, but it cannot be them as such.

In 'Kabbalah" apparently what or who is called the "guardian Angel" is translated as the Universal Self, but their self is not the Creator, is not Reality. It would be difficult to give a guardian angel the creative quality, the Reality quality. So according to the "Kabbalah" idea the warrior god must be the creator, although the idea of the Creator and war cannot be put in the same bed rationally. The creator needs to do no wars with its creations The Creator knows better. The Creator is above all.

PATHOS AND SCHOOLS

I am thinking of the Killing in the schools, the colleges and the universities. We remember what happened in Columbine High School where one student killed many Students and self, university of Montreal where Lepine sent to death a number of women. The Russian authorities had to the terrorist in "Chechenia" including many pupils in the school where the separatists took refuge. It is terrible violence in the schools. I hope it would never happen again. Yes it is the reflection of what is happening in the society at large. However, that is not all, the violence in the schools is telling us also that what we are actually teaching in the schools and the way we are teaching them are wrong. It is like violating the mind to teach the wrong thing, the wrong way with wrong attitude toward life in general.

I started to teach in Haiti. At that time hitting pupils were not considered as violating their sense of personhood. Recently, about a week ago (to day is Thursday June 17, 2010), it was on TV, a teacher angrily and frantically beating a child. According to me this is not the act of a gentleman neither of bravery. If another adult, able to replicate, were involved, the teacher would think twice before starting the beating act. I published the article in the Internet; I have read the content of the subject in the book written By Alvin R. Mahrer Ph. D. called Experiencing, A Humanistic Theory of Psychology and Psychiatry. What I published in the Internet is called "Effectance" Training, which is effectively done with an infant of about 3 months old till about a year old, so still too young for school. Nonetheless the attitude and the idea behind the "effectance" training. That is to say the child will know more and better about his life and his environment if helped to develop his self and sense of personhood than if he is not. This kind of attitude will do in any kind of school, will help prevent violence in the schools, and find better solutions to more difficult human problems. At colleges and universities the accent will be put in the application of the person sense of self and personhood to the problem to solve.

In the meantime, we can start by teaching intelligent morality courses to students from grade 7, if not earlier (Of the kind "La vertu sans argent n'est qu'un meuble inutile de Boileau-" virtue without money is a useless furniture—and "Boni bonum publicum current"—Good HBBs take care of public goods—keeping in mind "l" homme n'est ni ange ni bête le malheur veut qui fait l'ange fait la bête—more or less "Man and Woman are neither angel, neither beast. Unfortunately who plays the angel plays the beast"—It would not be thought by a religious person. They are teaching us all the time there is still violence at the school and elsewhere. The economy in general is very unstable. The moral and Creator familiarization courses (the development of the sense equality among all human beings is to be included also in this course) could be thought by a special psychologist or a qualified. Lay and honest person.

In the article I published in the Internet when the economy was at its lowest level, I said that part of the cause was because we became ideally bankrupt. Yes there are new gadgets all the time, but that is in technology. What we usually take for new ideas is frequently a repeat of history. In writing the article I was thinking at that time that the getting away from the Creator was itself behind the lack of ideas. Today I still think the same; still I add catastrophes, violence, famine with the economic crash, and morally and spiritually bankrupt to ideally bankrupt already in the article.

In other words we need to create a society where spirituality or the interest in our Creator is more pervasive. It could be done in many ways, however the one I have in mind now is the following:

First, plus the teaching of the course on intelligent morality in the school, we need to add a 30 minutes of meditation during the day class of all students from grade 1 to universities included in curriculum. The grade one pupil and the college or university student have 30 minutes during which the stay sitting in a relaxed fashion thinking of what ever comes to their mind, their own goals and desires without talking to anyone else around. In the intelligent moral course they will already have the background on meditation and on the interest on the creator. It is not a pure spirituality or materialism, just a bit more spirituality.

Second, although by now most of the workers are already familiar with mediation and the Creator, still it is to be installed in their work (all sorts of work, from the construction work to hospital, school and university work) days as well. At this time in our lives we do not necessarily need the intelligent and moral course, although the 30 minutes of meditation are necessary. There is no need of a content at that age; it is sufficient to just let them know that the 30 minutes is to think of themselves and the Creator. In that way the questioning of the creator will become a common fact in the whole society and all societies of the world. Spirituality level will be raised, and that will spare the world of a lot of headaches.

To raise the spirituality level I do not mention the method I use which is writing my DPs as soon as I have them and work with them later in order to comprehend them. It seems to me that this method would be impractical, even impossible to the majority of you to apply, It is difficulty to have to wake up many times at night to write DPs when you have to be at work at early in the morning for 8 or 9 hours. When I was teaching, started sleeping in the bus after class so much I was tired. For having to wake up about 4 in the morning. And the comprehension of the DPs during the day takes time.

In that way we will be individuals who can take their own lives in their own hands, and individuals who have a great deal of self respect and respect for others.

Now I am thinking that effectance Training course can be taught at any school from grade 7, not to develop the sense of self of these student. It may too late for that with them, but in order to prepare them so they can teach the ability to their own babies when they start their own parenting journey. This way they next generation of HBBs in the world will all have a sense self developed enough to take control of their lives, When everybody is brought up like that, 3 quarters of the problem world will vanish if not 90 to 95%. No need to walk on the others feeling because we cannot control ours, no need to steel the other person's car, we know how to create one or how to find money to buy one. We have confidence in ourselves and know that we can be as good as the other person in a few things though rhea may be different things, so the need for crime and violence will dramatically diminish.

In a DP recently, I had a teacher telling me that the situation I describe in school or the necessity for the intelligent moral course and the effectance-training course was when I was teaching, alluding that it is not there anymore. I bet the situation is the same if not even worse. There are still a lot of crimes being committed in all societies right now. Among them there are a lot drop out. So they are in crimes not only because they do not have enough skills but also because the schools fail to teach the proper courses that would keep them at school.

COMPULSION

I call them compulsion, Although it is not quite clear what the concept means exactly. The idea is a compulsion if we do not like it, if is strange, if it is new, if it makes us fill uncomfortable, because most of the time they come from the conditioning field. That is to say they come from individuals forcing us to live like HBBs lived traditionally. Obviously if the compulsion is a new idea, we will welcome it even if it creates negative feelings. W would call it rather an intuition.

MANIPULATION OF HBBS VIA TBS

The part that is really annoying when we use transcendental behaviors relates to manipulation. It is similar to conditioning. After I started the experiment in telepathy a big number of individuals contact me via direct communication or DP. Some of them gave me advices that I take for whatever it worth. It is only recently I discover that the big majority of them are manipulating me to accept their ideas, their ways of living, and their perspective in life. They are telling me when I should be mad, happy regardless the circumstances in the complete life. It is irritating at least to know someone who is not myself, do not know anything about me is determining me, telling me how to be and who to be.

However, the manipulation is nothing surprising. It is the bread and butter of society in general. There is always one group manipulating another for power and control. It is not quite the same as individual putting themselves in vulnerable situation and so are controlled by others as indicated previously. Those groups are somehow created by us to manipulate us. The priests, the doctors, the judges, the lawyers they are all fulfilling a sordid manipulative mission to keep us straight, in line with the rest of the society like zombies or slaves, whether or not they are conscious of that.

This state of affair could be multiplied in a million when we can use transcendental behaviors. We have more than one unusual channel of communication to complicate the manipulating situation. The ones who try to modify me are not necessarily doing it purposely, not necessarily conscious of what they are doing. They are living their lives as usual, but in this kind of life the institutions are set up for one person to determine another. Like the bisexuals in this house they behave as if they have an important mission to convert me into their bisexuality. They go at it forcefully because they are convinced it is the best way to live. Everyone has to be like everyone else, cannot be himself or herself. When a psychic girlfriend criticizes another woman. It is clear that she is jealous of the other woman. One someone else is doing it the person is in a mission. Fortunately when we are in the process of integration, when we can really use the TBs, the manipulation. Right now I could have million manipulative thought, they would have no effect on me whatsoever.

Forcing HBB to act differently than what he she intends to do, according to his her way can have grave consequences. It is not sure yet how the plane from Poland to Russia the second week of April 2010 made an accident and killing 94 HBBs including the President of Poland and his wife, including many other government officials. What is sure is that the pilot was probably forced to go ahead despite that he was told many times to divert the plane because it was in a foggy situation by Hobbs in tower control. They probably felt that they were government officials that they did not have to obey any one, even HBBs in a plane tower control, like they do usually on ground, forgetting that the rule of nature are un-abiding. They over ruled human laws.

The homosexual said to me this week in DP that he knows that I am lying about my sexual preferences, meaning that I am also a homosexual. My answer to that was he is crazy, only a crazy person would say that.

I did understand something about homosexuality recently. I read the idea in the Power of Empathy; I spent at least one hour in before I could develop it. It is that identification with the opposite sex, meaning the woman who identifies with his father will have crush for women, because his father loves woman. Likewise the man who identifies with his mother will have crush for men, because his mother likes man. Oh course they could also identify with same sex parent, then there is no homosexuality. Put that way (I was going to say pitted that way) it is a very logical explanation of the phenomenon called homosexuality.

Then the woman who identifies with her father, does she feels that her mother is an inferior being in comparison to her father, or does she think that women in general are inferior being in comparison to men?

Last night (April 16, 2010) I had a DP that I hit someone with a rock in his head . . . September 9, 2010, it was in the news a bear was charging a baseball man who hit the bear with a rock thrown at it face. I am not sure if the news is true, a bit similar with the DP.

His first name is Peter, a reminder of the words in the bible "Peter you are a rock, On this rock, I am going to build my church". Jesus Christ supposedly said these words. According to history he was killed because of his ideas. As human being we can sympathize with him on that. However I had a Quantity of DPs on him, in one of them he appeared nude suggesting homosexuality.

Last night I was supposedly to get ride of his energy in my psyche. For one reason I am no longer a religious person going to church.

I am promoting our Creator, via HBBs returning to themselves using their own-most: their body soul and spirit in order to ground the creator's truth, meaning that I do not know what others' truths will be even mine after all, still they will be necessarily different than mine. So sect, church, group's concept is certainly not in my mind, although I think that the individual is a social unit.

The Catholic Church is in trouble nowadays, because they are following metaphysics ideas: absolute concept, absolute form, as in the Western world where everything is calculated, "presencing" becomes the actual. Eternal return, where "technicity" is the end of knowledge etc. In that context knowing it all in advance, there is no possibility, no necessity for inquiring into the truth of the creator, knowing is knowing HBB's and things physical aspect only. In that sense, we are drifting away from our creator, left alone with ourselves to our risk and peril. To our disappearance ultimately. It is the real way to get ourselves in trouble, not just by the atomic bomb.

The churches are applying occidental metaphysics, which itself is a translation of Greek's metaphysics mistake. As indicated above we all do our best, although we are lost in translation, although sometimes doing our best can bring us straight to catastrophe.

I do not know eastern metaphysics much. I do know that most of the Arabic countries may be under the influence of Buddha's teaching in which the renouncing concept is central and applied. Any way life as it is now does not let us think that eastern philosophies are any better than western philosophies, Eastern practice with extremist killing (Air India), with honor killing (members of family to keep its good name) with long war in Palestine. All these events suggest rather that the HBBs in the eastern part of the world too are drifting away from our Creator little by little.

Any way "I will build my church" can be translated as grounding the truth of our Creator. In other words by now I am supposed to ground a creator's truth although I haven't got the slightest idea yet what that truth could be. The earthquake in Tibet where Dalai Lama lives, the trouble in the Catholic Church make me think, but I made no conclusion.

The DP above reminds me also of that when we dwell in our creator field, there are solicitations by the gods to create all sorts of structures of phenomena, including creating a church, a religion, the idea in psychology is the gods know all the structures of all life phenomena

The big churches such as Catholicism, Adventist fail in that they do nothing to get us close to our Creator, to getting us to observe it in order to ground its truth. The small religions such as Witchcraft, Neo-paganism, Shamanism and so on by now would develop and get us to observe our creator if the big religions did not to strangle them. The persecution of Witches is well known historical fact. At a certain point in time, the persecution was consecrated by the Witchcraft Act in England in 1735. It took more than 2 centuries before it got repealed in 1951 The act was one of the negative events that block the progression of spirituality in human life and at the same time taking us away from our Creator.

How did it get to the Witch-hunt? Pope Innocent V111 in 15th Century declared witchcraft an heresy, the biggest sin of all. Before that the religious HBBs were saying that witchcraft did not exist. This religious negative attitude toward small religions was not manifested just in regard to witchcraft. In the big religions members were ready to kill anyone who did not agree with there theories. That is how there was the Crusaders war. Yap, If you do not agree with me I am going to kill you, even if we are both religious. That is why it suggested above if each individual does make any effort to change things around, does not watch our Creator, does let every spiritual activity be decided by the big religions, decision that will take us directly to abyss.

And that does not require any worshiping, living an authentic life with the creator, as part of it is already worshiping enough.

MY VERSION OF CREATION OF ALL

By the way, to place things in perspective, to be able to live not in a vacuum but in some sort of structure, I think <u>that first: there is our Creator, second: the nothingness, third: the gods/ goddesses (and pathologies created by the needs of the creator), fourth: the nature (structure and unstructured) and fifth HBBs.</u>, There can be more items to place in between the five categories, however the order of the categories should stay the same. Anyway it is the spiritual frame in which I operate and it is my version of creation. I do not know anybody, any nation of HBBs in the past or now who conceive the existence this way. And I see it this way thanks to the research in psychokinetic telepathy.

In Comparison here is what is Gurdjief' called Ray of creation in the Book Hidden Wisdom:

Absolute
All world (nature)
All Suns (nature)
Sun (nature)
Moon (nature)

The brackets are mine to underline the fact in his version of creation almost all the items are about nature. In other parts of the book the author describe his actions as done by a spiritual person. However is version of creation is a total materialistic endeavor. I suppose the word absolute is there for the Creator, still there is no nothingness, no gods, no HBBs. I already mentioned that the concept absolute reminds me of ceramic, so I would not use it to indicate the Creator who is incomplete life, infinite almost the opposite of absolutism. With this version of creation we are not out of the wood yet.

I do not know the religious versions, but is clear in theirs there is the fundamental error of confusing the gods with the Creator.

Thinking of god, nature is thinking of creation, it is not thinking of the Creator. I can create a pencil, thinking of the pencil is not thinking of me

After all, Realty or the Universal Self is not really comprehensible by humans. We make theories on it in order to figure out who we are, but these theories are pertinent to ourselves not to Reality itself. Being created by our Creator does not in itself give us any claim on the understanding on understanding it completely, there is nothing to compare it with anyway, but we can observe it to ground its truth related to, which will almost always be relative and related to observer. The Creator is in the incomplete life level. Whether we want it or not our comprehension of it will stay incomplete it is what I am really trying to say.

Jesus Christ and the religious leaders of the other races are in the range of archetypes or gods more likely.

The creator is unnamable, untouchable unapproachable as such, Nonetheless Creator or Universal Self or Reality, those names are the best and the most sure ways to indicate it, in order not to make mistake. God is the worst way to indicate it and a bit of a put down, given that god is a creation its creation and is referring to male only. It would have to be god, goddesses and thing, then we would not get out of the would yet.

Guardian Angel seems to be the name given to the Creator in the ancient religions and across history, but it is unlikely that Guardian was recognized as such, was then consciously associated with the Universal Self or Reality.

My position in the psychological landscape is closer to Gnostics, so I am further away from the agnostics according to whom God (I suppose they mean the Creator) cannot be known directly by an individual. On the contrary, the Gnostics affirm that it is possible to directly know God or the Creator. I am in that side of their thinking and say rather that the Creator is in each individual and each thing (I saw what I believed to be the Creator in DP, this is not a claim that I understand it, but a claim that I know It a little bit, although the thinking of the Gnostics is a bit muddy for in their thinking there is a confusion as to who is God, because no distinction is made between the Creator or Universal Self or Reality and the gods and goddesses as I did in my version of creation above. There are many gods and goddesses who are created by the Universal Self. Sophia is the Goddess wisdom, apparently there are god and goddess of nature, in French they say Dame nature, The soul and the spirit are also of the domain of the gods and goddesses (similar to the archetypes of Jung). The distinction between the Creator and the gods and goddesses is small, however make it hugely clearer to us when we are dealing with creation.

After all we know we cannot know much about creation, being one ourselves, in the same way we cannot really know the structure of our galaxy be cause we are in it. Still we cannot know creation more than the Creator can't; still we need to live with a theory, unless we want to be in the crazy bunch, of what we think the existence is, on how we come to be on earth. In other words mine is one theory among others.

Nowadays it is like committing a crime to mention the Creator to someone else. It would be better to talk about the computer and sport, which are nothing bad in themselves. I suspect that the confusion in regard to the Creator and the creation put disillusion in us, one of the causal elements in the-getting-away-from-the-Creator. The disillusion is nourished by the confusion. It is a fundamental hiccup, which seems to be with us from the beginning of HBBs' life on earth.

It is obvious that I am not a religious person, although I was born in catholic religion. Sometimes I meet HBBs they start to talk to me about Voodoo or Vaudou in French and creole, or they talk to me about Witchcraft. To my surprise these religions are also interested in the Creator. To the 2 above we can add Alchemist religion, American Indian religion, 'Kabbalism" Magic, Shamanism. Before I thought magic behavior consisted only of individual doing tricks like cutting HBBs in Boxes in two while they are still alive and in one piece. Now I know the "truckers" form only a minority of magicians 2 to 3%. The big majority of magicians is interested in Realty or our Creator and shows that way a very humanistic side of themselves.

Here is a bit on how they are described in the book Hidden Wisdom: "The magician concerned with reaching the divine, using the most direct path, everything else is a mere distraction" . . . The occultist or the magician, not only to view the landscape, but to interact with it as well. There is the side of Western Metaphysics in this book, so I was skeptical for a moment. At the end I decided knowledge is knowledge, that it does not matter much where we find it, then I read the book.

Violet Firth (1890-1946) founded an occult lodge called the Society of the Inner Lights, Which still operates in London. I have entered this in my computer in a spot I call 'Bilan" in it I write what I have read as memory. Before yesterday, Wednesday, June 2, 2010 the taxi driver went "basuk" killed many HBBs in London and himself, despite a very effective Gun controlled program in England. I think it is a very strange coincidence that it happened exactly while I am writing about the world of magician. It underlined the accuracy and the power of my type of science.

According to the book magic is in a neutral zone; it can be used for positive or negative purposes. One thing is certainly going for those of small or ancient religious groups, I mean they all focus on "relativilization" of the ego to get close to the Creator. In contrast the big religion focus on monotheism and the ego. With in mind that religion is something universal, that we all do it in a way

NEW AGE MOVEMENT

The research I am doing could be classified in the New Age movement if it was necessary, although I have very little knowledge of the group. It is said that the New Age group is very popular in North America. According to a study done in 1990, 4 billions $ a year are spent in New Age consultant, enormous amount in workshops and seminars; 30 billions $ are spent on business training; enormous amount is disbursed for courses, treatments aromatherapy, books and magazines.

Besides him (Alvin Mahrer, page 65), there was Alice Baily (1880-1949), she was the one who started to talk about the New Age movement and material transported through human beings (similar to transcendental behaviors), she did say, I believed, that she received a message while very far apart from a Tibetan Monk who claimed to be alive. So the possibility was in there for her to discover the transcendental behaviors, it was in the psychology field also. As said above it was buried under psychological dust, especially when anything connected to the spiritual can be connected also to the mental, it can be wrongly associated also to the mentalist, an horror for the so called scientific psychologist, taking at the same time the transcendental behaviors away from the psychological field.

The way I describe it is a soft fashion to take a step back from New Age psychology conceptually speaking. All in all, I am saying to myself with all this popularity, I do not see any progress in raising the spirituality level of the world, in fact I notice instead rush back to pure materialism and empty-ness, a galloping back to oblivion. If the new age popularity is not for more spirituality does not bring us to the observation of our Creator, what is it for then? What is the reason of its tastiness it is clear to us now that despite the step back of humanity in regard to our Creator, there is at the same time a thirsty-ness for it that my version of creation may help to reduce by getting colder to it?

I notice also sometimes in the morning I wake up with a hurt in my wrist or in my foot, which force me to take pills that put me in a more like trance state. I do not need altered state of consciousness, except sleep, nor to be possessed as in certain religion, as in Voodoo, nor speak in languages as in certain churches. The wake up in trance like state is from the ego, my black colored ancestors. I have terrible headache in the weekend sometimes, when I slow down the studies in the weekend when I do less of them. It must be in the range of the same explanation, the trance like state HBBs have in certain religion, which I do not need at all.

After all the small religions such Witchcraft, Neo-paganism, and Kabbalah have a conception of the Creator very similar than mine according to the way it is summarized in the book Hidden Wisdom: "They regard the source of all things as being un-namable, non-manifested"(incomplete as written above). To these adjective I would add, fluid, pure, untouchable, unapproachable, according to ma vision of it (Each time I tried to approach it and touch it, it escaped and appeared at another place in the room.

GOD OR NOT

My father's first name was Soys, my mother's Eucaris. Soys can be thought as soi or self in English. There is the legend of transformation named Euchacarist that is used in the Christian religion. Both of them are born in a very small village named Dieurond like round god in English. When I was very young about 7 chronological years old, Seradieu (it will be god) the son of a neighbor hit me in the eye with a rock. And we have just qualified using the TB as being in the divine field. Would I be qualified for the god position? According to the archetypal psychology the gods are in distant places closer to the Creator. So human is disqualified, even after death, it's like. However I do have supernatural powers to stop wars and do many extraordinary things (with a huge sense of responsibility). That does not mean it is a power I can consciously control it yet.

All in all the notion of hidden masters governing the spiritual evolution of humanity had entered popular consciousness, according to the book Hidden Wisdom, a long time ago thanks to a woman Helena Blavotsky (1831-1891), that is to say I am may be one of these masters or I may become one of them. For the moment I can barely remember my name sometimes. That reminds us of the story of a woman who had to pass an exam. She did it with the highest mark, but she could not remember her name for about 20 minutes.

Yesterday in a DP I saw myself with a woman I called Monise, the first name of my sister, Cedieu, who was working for my father at one time, was with a woman I call Mercida, another woman my father had, for me she symbolizes Avril. Some how the name Cedieu (translation: this is god) may be similar to the Da-sein of Heidegger made it so that Mercida switched place with Monise in the DP. So Mercida came to be with me and Monise goes with Cedieu who was still limping on a foot. I do not quite understand the DP yet, but it seems to be something related to the gods and Da-sein. Monise being my sister's first name, even if it is just a metaphor I was not attracted to her sexually. It was not the same for Mercida or Avril. Who knows what?

When we are making decision all advices we get via they transcendental behaviours are to be judged before we accept them. We have to find out if the solution resonates with the rest of our lives. DP seems to be the best advisor, because we are almost completely unconscious. Our plan is made consciously and we will do better to stick to it as much as possible (there so many suggestions from conditioning field, they are sometimes negative).

CREATIVE DPS

There are many ways to deal with the psychic invasion. There must be a common point, HBBs you like even indirectly with the slightest liking. Before I use to kill the energy in the psyche, that is, with the intention not to get bugged by the person. It is indicated above that I was in fight with Daniel who was following me during DP. It is already indicated also that it is easier to extinguish a DP by not reinforcing it, not trying to understand it, not trying to write about it. As it is not that easy to extinguish a direct communication, the third way was to deal with the psychic invasion is by getting mad at it during DP. At that moment we are only one step away from what I baptized as creative DPs, to be able to create something in our lives.

The other step as simple as the first step is to have a couple man and woman in the DP, then getting mad at a situation and or another person. In other words it is creating by love (couple) in the DP.

As indicated above war can be stopped, nations can be liberated that way. Who would think that we can stop war by love, not love in lalaland, but love in incomplete and in complete life love and sexualitlity.

DIFFICULTY TO FALL IN LOVE

It is Because we do not have anymore two important elements conducive to falling in love which are the sense of loneliness and worthlessness. Yes, the existential feeling of being lonely and worthless disappears with the ability to use of the transcendental behaviors. Instead of feeling lonely sometime we can even feel being invaded by so many HBBs speaking to us via transcendental communication. There is no possibility anymore of feeling lonely.

Then with the TBs, as said above and sown. We have value brought in us in part by that we are able to get in touch with practically any one in the world, rich poor, powerful, non powerful, famous non famous. Also we have a sense that we can do extraordinary things, as you will see on the goodies in the next chapter. Those characteristics valuate us.

However they are necessary to fall in love. I can take myself as example; I spent 12 years without a woman, meaning without love and sexual actives from 1998 to now 2010. Although I always want to create that in my life I always need to love. I have many women friend in psyche, but they too are under the spell of the transcendental behavior in the sense that they are no longer feeling lonely and worthless or they no longer have a profound sense of worthlessness and loneliness. So those psychic friends or girlfriends make no move to meet me in the complete life situation, they just park in my psyche. It is the problem we have when we are able to use the TBs.

Chapter 6

GOODIES as RELATED TO TBs

COMPANY AS OPPOSED TO SOLITUDE

Obviously we cannot be alone when we can use the transcendental behaviors. We always have someone wanting to communicate with us via direct perception or communication, In that sense we can say that there are a lot of lot of HBBs out there using the transcendental behaviors unknowingly and that we can be alone only in complete physical life. It is not clear how the concept solitude came to life, we human must have a sense that it is impossible to be alone completely.

A SENSE OF INNER POWER—OF CREATING LIFE AROUND US

I am thinking of the number of films TV shows inspired by the research in psychokinetic telepathy. It is one way I think of inner power with the transcendental behavior, Surely I did not meet the creator of these films, TV series or stories, meaning that we must have been communicating or experiencing via the transcendental behaviors or indirectly especially from women I met that way. I am thinking of Donald Trump's daughter, Evanka, whom I used to meet in psyche a few times when the Apprentice was about to air.

When I do not have too much money, there is often food on sale in the store where I usually buy food as well as in the store where I buy cloths. I was going to the Vancouver Central library without eating. Close to the library there is a restaurant on Homer Street Close To Robson Street, the restoration person I never met before came to meet me on the street offering food.

The bedroom in which I am living now looks like it has been furnished for the research, for me with a bed lamp with a special button which makes it easier to light the lamp at night to write DPs.

We have a lot influence on life, the environment via the transcendental behaviors, meaning we influence not only other HBBs but also things, and phenomenon such as hurricane, earthquake and the like.

CREATIVE POWER

That is I am colLecting evidence of the points I want to make right there in nature. I only have to listen to the news to find them. They are in this book. I do not have to reminisce about them. I think without abstraction, without having to force the subject to prove a point I have in mind in advance, already proven. That reminds me of another brother who past away. Before his death, I saw someone with a lot of blood on his head, After his death they say he had a brain tumor. I do not have to describe his whole character here, but lately or before his death, he was very busy with the Catholic Church where there is one god, living alone the creator, where they apply the wrong metaphysics. No wonder he had a brain tumor, forcefully proving egocentric monotheism.

When I have my ideas, I am not even quite awake. I cannot torture my brain to have them. My life is an amalgamation of incomplete and complete life events. I let myself guided by the phenomenon I am studying and by god or goddess knowing the structure of the phenomenon.

I get the impression that I awake the ability to use the transcendental behaviors in many HBBs I meet in the street, in buses via the TB and almost everybody I get in touch with physically or psychically. They start to communicate with me quite naturally transcendentally, although it is only me who know consciously about the transcendental behavior and who start to write about them. The girl in this house is mathematician, but we communicate transcendentally quite naturally to the point that only us know what we feel about each other, only us know each other that well. I have the impression that we were in that kind of communication even before we came to live in this house. So we have met on DP before she move in this house

So I may awake in most HBBs I meet the ability to use the transcendental behaviors. What I do not know is if they are using the ability between themselves, if these individuals can communicate directly between themselves without me being the third person through which the communication pass through, if the they have DPs between themselves, direct experiences between themselves. I know they communicate with each other in my space of the psyche, girls try to pick boys in my psyche, and guys try to pick girls in my psyche. That is what brings the question up: Are they using the ability between themselves? Any which way, I feel that our world will never be the same again. The little experiment in telepathy will have profound impact. On new civilization.

The DP that would corroborate my statement in regard to these experiences is the following: I put my hand on top of what looks dry leaves on the floor. on top of them but not touching them. They elevate as a small plant. I did it many times with the same result. I had a woman with me, I asked her to watch me doing it.

MY DISCOVERIES IN MEDICINE

After the house I was living was sold, I had to move to a hotel for a month. Let's say it was not a very convenient living there. Later I move to another place, ended up with some health issues. The most prominent one was that I could not move my left arm, and I had a terrible pain in the lung on the same side. Saint Paul hospital could not help me with that. Later I discovered that it was what I called multi-organic disease, what is called la gout or arthritis. So I took the same medicine given to treat this sickness for my pain in the lung and the pain was gone.

Then I was having my heart beating irregularly a few time I thought that it must have been the same kind on thing, so I took Novo methacin given to treat arthritis. The heart became normal afterward, although sometimes I forgot the equation and took the pill late may be because the pills itself has some side effects as one physician mentioned once.

From September to November of last year 2009, I lived in five places, not very careful about what I was eating. I went to the doctors in the West-End Walking Clinic. They made me make the tests; I had high blood pressure, and to elevated rate of cholesterol in my blood stream. They gave me pills to take them down; I had to go to the same place one day to take heart-beating measure. The senior Ned, the doctor told me that I was going to have a heart attack. The day after a Sunday, at the sink in the kitchen I felt the same "arrhythmia" I used to feel and took the Novo-methacin for it. Then the heartbeat became normal, still a bit more elevated than normal 120 beats per minute. But the point is the "Arrhythmia" I was having is the same as swollen foot, joint sicknesses in general. I explained that to the doctor, he look surprised, however who can talk against hard fact. It is my discovery in medicine; I baptized it "multi-organic disease". It looks like a concentrated energy in circulation in the body and which attacks the organs that are overworked, or sick somehow. This kind of multi-organic malady may be linked to what Charles T, Tart called "kundalini" the energy in our back assimilated to a snake (is that about the nerves system?) and it may manifest itself a little bit differently in each individual. I have a great deal of DPs on snake.

May be even the functional diseases such as Alzheimer, Parkinson are also the same sickness as the so called gout and could be treated with gout medicine, Although functional diseases seem to be more like a mental problem and could be best treated by therapy to sort out the functions for the patient who confuses mind with brain and brain with spirit etc, Because it is more a disease of the less younger chronological age bracket, it may be to late for this learning to be effective. In other words it would be better for all to learn to differentiate the body and the mental functions at school in order not to have something like Parkinson disease later in life.

Having DP everyday, my heart works a lot. The observation is there is heart bit irregularity during DP

What I called the multi-organic disease may be not a disease at all, after all. The body changes itself each second. These second changes accumulate to have a new organ in a year or so. At that time we may suffer pain. So what we usually called illness may simply be a growing pain or something similar. It is said that the organs such as the heart, the nerves do not renew themselves. My being says that says that some heart diseases may play the same renewing functions.

RIDES ON THE FACE

Somebody says on TV that the line in our face are the results of the sun rays, giving the example that we do not have lines in any other covered parts of our body, and she was talking according to a research. It is a very simplistic research. For there are many more coming in the causal factorization of rides in the face?

First of all we may elucidate that rides in the face is not sickness but it is a fancy of human being not to have them in the face. Second elucidation is that the children do not have ride on the face except in rare situation. So rides come with chronological age (from young adult and up).

I count many facts that may cause rides on the face; 1) is mastication, it would explain the fact that children do not have rides on the face; 2) the sun rays; 3) center of gravity, still explains why children do not have them; 4) laughing, children are to young to laugh to the rides on the face; 5) the curtains the windows which have pleats, Francophone would have them even if it was not a physical factor for the equivalent for the word is rideau, part of it is ride, our mind would be reflecting them in our face in later life period; 6) looking at ourselves in the mirror we pull back our face automatically so creating rides; 7) we forget our face most of the time, a face that cannot see itself without a mirror; 8) durable physical and psychological pain; 9) by compulsion, so it would be genetic, compulsion such as "panneau-pli" (pli for rides); 9)spider or picture of spider in DP.; I have red a book "The life of the Mind: by Hanna Arendt, after that I kept seeing the picture of a spider in DP; 10) the absence of emotion meaning the absence of soul.

The questions are relevant above all to the physical beauty industry; especially to some psychic friends I have as Milla, Julia in Maybelline and many nice ladies I saw on TV advertising beauty product. Letting it all go by itself, some discipline with our body may spill into our soul and spirit. We would then put body, soul and spirit in causal and circular relation.

Cigarette, cigar, pipe smoke can be a factor causing rides on the face also. Trying to prevent smoke from these products to go to our eyes we close them a bit making at the same time some rides in our face.

Why is that HBBs with a round face do not have rides on their face a lot as angular face do? And why the fuss about rides in the face?

The round face HBB of course does not have rides in the face. The rides are straight lines. There are not quite round lines. They also have more flesh and its derivative in his or her face. Then round or straight face face with rides or face without rides, big face small face with or without a face, docs it matter. We already have here part the answer of the second question. We fuss about the rides on the face because it is the mark of being less younger, which reminds us of last days of life, of death. Human beings are only stigmatized that way, for we die at any chronological age. So rides are at least not the only sign of nearing death. Then I am saying it again there is no logical explanation for dying at a certain age, given that our cells are renewing themselves and that in some special case children have the face with rides eighth the so-called body. Body elements renewed themselves each second at the elemental level.

After all face is our physical identity, the door to our soul (like the things we see are the door to the Soul of the World), there is an aesthetic connotation to the human face. Furthermore, sometimes having a good pleasant nice looking face is required, especially when we are working in the entertainment industry.

Sometimes I crave watching the fashion shows. There would be a bit of genetic impulse there; my grand father of the mother side was a tailor. At the beginning I wanted to watch the young ladies there, later I discovered that there is a deeper aesthetic sense in me, probably after the big number of images I have whilst using the imaginative ability to create my goals. It is not a waste of time to cultivate external beauty and dressing the body to elevate its standing in the eye of everybody, given that it is the best vehicle we can ever have, given that it is disregarded in some religion who knows from what theory, given that there could be a link between the beauty of the body well dressed and the beauty inside of the person.

At the same time we cannot exaggerate in this field of beauty either. Some Philosophers think that everything made by the Creator is beautiful. This week there was at Oprah a woman having a balloon on her face a kind of tumor. Each time the doctors cut it, it came right back again. The physician said that it was genetic. If the cause was known they would know equally how to treat it Nonetheless the "ugliness" outside may also be revealing the ugliness inside, after being to fussy about beauty. Also it is a sign/ of HBBs very. Disintegrated.

After all, I do not know the fashion industry at all, if the young ladies are mistreated or not.

A similar equation can be made about being to fussy about sport and the ravage it makes on human beings' body sometimes. It is ok to do sport to keep being healthy, however the commercial sport pushing HBBs to do sport without rhyme or reason is not healthy at all according to me. It is killing them; it is taking an arm, a foot, and a back from them for no healthy purposes. And keeping them away from their soul anyway.

PROPOSITION TO USE THE TBS FOR HEALING

The subject is as thin as an egg shell, for in this life there are institutions which are manufacturing sicknesses, there are groups who are manufacturing sicknesses, involuntarily most of the time, the individuals who are sick participate in creating their own sicknesses. As I already wrote elsewhere, all the employees of a hospital who do they like best deeply, a healthy person who is never sick, or someone who is sick all the times? The answer has to be the person who is ill often, because this way they can keep their job. It is not the fault of the patient neither the healer. Life is that way, However if everyone can be him or herself, the bad side of this life can be reduced. If we are alienated in these circumstances, we are in for a rough ride.

That said, now with the transcendental behaviors uncovered we have a tool to go beyond the apparent disorders with the patient in order to come up with the right treatment. My comprehension of the healing process is a bit similar to what is in the book Experiencing. The problems are repress potentials seeking a way of expression. The role of the therapist is not to push them down to please society, a way to kill the person anyway (inside), but to let the door wide open to them so they can come out in their positive form. There is a difference between the treatment in the book and my proposition of treatment for the good reason that no one was talking about transcendental behaviors before me, before the research on telepathy

May be it is not appropriate to ask a therapist to right down his DP everyday to get an insight in the patient problem, still, direct communication, direct experience and direct perception make it possible to get spirit to spirit (soul to soul) communication with him or her part of the patient that knows almost all about him or her. The transcendental behaviors are love behaviors, they happen in intimate level. The kind of healing I am proposing is love treatment or treatment by love in that sense.

Saying the person is mentally sick, is crazy, unknowingly or with knowing awareness, using these words loaded with negative connotation is a bad start for she can be only unstructured mentally and or physically by herself only or by herself in connivance with the environment. That can lock the door on the face of the most clever intention and cure.

THE COURAGE OF NATURE

When we can use transcendental behaviors, we do not have the fear of nature, neither unusual fear when we are confronted by natural events. Direct perception is done at sleep, no place for real fear there. The same goes for direct experiences also, given that they also occur mostly during sleep. In direct communication we are awake but not in complete life, so there is any danger there. We are communicating via body cells and or via spirit. That is the first part the argument. The second part is that when we are dealing with the transcendental behaviors, we are as close to Reality, our Creator as we can get. At that moment we transcend nature as such, thus no fear of it, no unusual fear of natural events. I notice some abnormal fear of nature and natural events twice recently.

First, the volcanic eruption in Iceland last week (Today is April 21, 2010), makes me think of the fear of nature in most of us probably due to exclusive materialism and thinking and or metaphysics heritage that the nature is the end of everything, there is no creator, no reality behind it, there is nothingness but it is negative one not a first step of things, still we are supposed to come from there. Everybody traveling in plane Europe last week must have been disturbed somehow, because most of the plane were grounded and the Airports were loosing 2 hundred million $ everyday, with the assumption that the ashes in the smoke in the air could seriously wreck the plane engine (volcanic ash from Iceland. After a few days they fly an empty plane in dark cloud nothing happened. After the test I started to think that there might be unusual fear behind the grounding of so many planes.

Second, that reminds me of other event, which occur after the earthquake in Haiti (but a 10 billion dollars gift from the generous world) last days of December 2009. Afterward I called my brother who left Haiti one day before the earthquake and who went back to New York where he lives. I call Italien afterward talked about the earthquake. I told him that I kind of knew beforehand that there was going to be an earthquake in Haiti and told him in what circumstances I made the prediction. He started to talk back to me wildly, I did not understand but we stopped talking abruptly. It was only later I realized that, he had the fear of me because of the foreseeing the quake, which is the fear of the quake and nature in general.

And worse that fear of nature is probably part of causality of some catastrophes themselves because the fear of nature ultimately means not knowing nature. Not being close to nature or not having nature in our inner world.

The problem in the Mexican Gulf with the oil-licking rig is another big events I cannot ignore during the redaction of this book. It started about 2 weeks from now (May 3, 2010). The gas linking in the sea is still happening, the leaked gas is getting further and further from the starting point of the leak and the human beings in the costal areas are worried. There are the pictures of big sea turtle covered of brut gasoline; quantities of them are covered with the stuff, the black oil. Fishermen are complaining that if something is not done to stop the move of the oil, there will be no fish to catch. In the news they call it ecological disaster despite that at the Oil Company BP, they seem to be doing their best to stop it.

It is something to witness how concerned the community is about the event. It means that negligent and fraudulent companies exploiting the gas beneath the sea will not be tolerated. President Obama spoke to the concerned HBBs about it in a tentative to calm them. This disaster is the result of human enterprise; nature has little to do with its cause, although the wind may make it difficult to manage the outward move of the oil. Then at the same time this afternoon it was presented on TV a company who can't keep up for its product, a kind of long red tube, a boom, to prevent the oil from moving to in the sea shore. The company sent one truck of the stuff everyday to the Mexican gulf, meaning that this company is making money, creating employment. So there is one good side to the event. The same weekend, many twisters in United States killing many individuals. At the same time there are floods destroying houses, chasing human beings away from their houses. One person says that "nature is mean to us in this area".

In the future the twisters could be redirected. Something could be done to canalized the flood path to avoid houses. It would take too much work to get it some may be. Certainly the houses could be built flood proof. I do not think that would take too much work to build houses at level above the floods or put a wall high around it (Where the water cannot reach) which happened every year, leaving us with a lot clues on its behaviors. It would take a desire and a law to do that. Some politician may think in the back of their mind that it is better to leave the situation the way it is now to create jobs. Isn't it?

Joke a part, after 86 days the state of affairs seems to be under control now (July 19-2010). Now the bird, the fish, other animals and especially living HBBs in the area, the Company BP and the American in general can breathe knowing that the spilling of the bad stuff in the sea stops. However what makes me write about it today is that I had a direct perception I start by washing some cloths in a kind of fountain. Some of the cloths get in the pipe, water pours out in the basin and I was a bit scared. Up to now it is a normal thing having a DP on the accident. But I was struck by that I had the DP only Saturday night, when the problem started to be solved (I have many direct the same way, when the problem is at its end anyway).

All along the days during which the spill continued, I felt that we were all responsible for what happened, that I should be able to help, I wanted to help them via DP, because I did not have any name of the BP's personnel to call. Saturday night to Sunday morning, in a DP, I have learned that the spilling is stopped and in another direct perception I dreamt something related to the problem in the gulf. The fact that the name gulf (similar to engulf) is used to indicate the area may play a part in causing the spilling.

I may had DP on it that when all my parts were too involved in it to remember the psychic experience; I may push the DP in the bottom of my memory for one reason or another; the company BP might want the problem to be solved by there engineers in order not to loose face, or somebody might unconsciously want the spilling to continue (reminds me of a certain Schreiber, I wanted to help keep her alive, I had a DP on her only after her death).

The same week, Steve Jobs (He mentioned to me that he feels frustrated, sucked in "technicity"), the CEO of Apple in communication said on TV that even his company had a little trouble with the new version of with the Phone (which make think I cold help this company with the service I offered to HBBs in the internet this month: Transcendental Counseling). However the point I want to make is this, reliance only on science by HBBs is dangerous, for the problem becomes more and more complicated. The other face of the statement is that living with Reality having a little space in our thinking by observing its truth and grounding it, by putting more spirituality in our lives seems to be the way to go.

Steve Jobs and the buyers of the new version of the Phone seem be having the metaphysical complex that is everything is absolute so everything must start perfectly all the time when little reason is telling us that most of the time the start is clumsy, stumbling, tottering, disorderly.

There is the zeal toward the nature, nature care takers nowadays: the wild life protector, the ecological protector, the environmental protector (we would not want to go back to horse time anyway) the ecosystem protector, the animal lover and so on. They constitute the right attitude toward nature. I do not know if that will help us a lot in the long run, if the aversion against reality continues. True, animals nature, the gods, the elements could get us close to the Creator if we were not aversive to Reality in the first place (deep down we are also aversive to nature). And, at all cases the way life is running right now contributes to the removal from Reality, despite our natural propensity to save ourselves, the earth. Also I guess we would fare better in times of natural and human caused disasters if things were the other way around, if we were observing reality to find what it brings to our lives, its truths.

There were giant animals roaming on the earth once, they disappear apparently all at once. The earth was all covered with ice once, then the ice disappear with some left in the poles. The sun is getting hotter and hotter, slowly but surely. We are behaving as if we know what it is all about, even though we do not know that. We do not know our Creator's plan.

I observed the same natural events were surfacing when I was writing the other books. When I was writing the Soul Exposed, many of them happened, Floods occur so regularly every year that it could be considered like a banal event, if there were no destruction of houses and lives, disasters as Exxon Valdez, Katrina, Mexican gulf gas leak are not the usual events. Nature and reality are attracting our attention on something wrong. That is how they are linked to the research in psychokinetic telepathy.

Then, there are the human beings who are forgotten by the rest of us and who happen to monopolize our attention when there is a natural disaster in their places. Forgetting human beings is also forgetting the creator and vice versa.

That kind of propensity toward nature does not seem to be real. At all cases we get more natural disasters and more complicated ones as that. Our feelings, ideas and actions will not be real in the absence of the Creator. Not being real we are living a dangerous life even with our good feelings. Good will toward nature. The accident in the highway last Sunday (today is Tuesday June 29, 2010) in British Columbia, in which 2 are dead, others injured were unfortunate but speak to that, the danger of fanaticism toward nature away from our Creator. The driver was trying to avoid passing over a duck and her chicks in the middle of the highway. She had good feelings; intention for the birds, still in this specific case keeping heirs and her friends lives would be a better course of action.

Heightened Experiencing

MahArer talks about it in his book experiencing A humanistic theory of psychology and Psychiatry. Apparently it is the purpose of life according to him is to have these experiences, they make us feel alive they come about after we have been integrated and actualised a bit. In some other school of psychology it is called pick experiences when our inner world is in harmony with or external world external world. The person using the transcendental behaviors is in the process of integration and actualization. It is why I mention the heightened experiences in this part of the book the goodies of transcendental behaviors.

The Most Intimate Experiencing

I remember making love once during direct perception with the first women that I admire, but instead of making love with her normally, I saw that I was making love to her flesh, I saw all her inside. It happened to me like that with a couple of women. I still do not know what that supposed to mean. May be it is an allusion to HBBs who make love to women and kill them. May be it is an allusion to the pejorative expression meet market, when we make love to HBBs we are not quite interested in or they make love to us without interested in us. I am puzzled by these experiences, however that is not the point. The point is that with the transcendental behaviors we make the most intimate experiences. Those are extreme, but they convey the idea. They remind me of the spider who has to eat its partner after mating.

The star has two kids each time I met her via the transcendental behaviors at her place I touch her belly, she runs away we laugh at it. It is only later I realized that I was touching her belly in DP to make her loose extra skin or fat in that area of her body after giving birth to two children. So, the transcendental intimacy can be useful too.

STOP WARS, LIBERATE NATIONS

One more goody we have when we use transcendental behaviors, we can stop wars and liberate nations. I did it unknowingly, unwillingly, spontaneously at a time when I was trying to make ends meet, now too, financially speaking. It is clear that I would not be thinking with such grandiosity. It is already indicated here, the deconstruction of the Berlin Wall, the liberation of the East European countries by the Soviet Union was the work of Raya a Russian lady I was going out with in Winnipeg, and Angelika a German lady I was going out with in same Winnipeg. They loved me, I loved them. We did not think or talk about the situation in Europe. We did not talk about politics. However, when we met, I had just finished a bachelor in linguistics at the University of Quebec in Montreal where they have a big political agenda. When I met Raya and Angelika, political ideas were still fresh in my mind (more details in Soul Exposed)

I still now have the same abilities, but this time I will use them consciously, meaning with judgment. I am not saying that it was not an important thing to throw cold water on the on the warrior attitude and the division of the world in 2 war blocs, the soviets leading one block and the Americans leading the other block within a cold war which was rather hot war, but somehow politely. It was an important thing to do, now I would do it if at the same time it helps to create my goals, personal and with worldly characteristics. I want to create a family. I am still not able to do that. So I have to use every minute of my time wisely.

And then, we might posture ourselves in a non intelligent moral podium and find that it is immoral to go out with many women, that we should marry just one woman, that polygamy is always a big difficulty. After that who would we think we are facing the particular problem between German HBBs and Russian HBBs to think like that? In other words it took me to go out with both Russian woman and the German one Angelica to sort out the issue. Yes, in most cases polygamy can cause suffering, for I myself have been some sort a victim of that, born from a father of at least 30 children made with many women. However, as you see, sometimes it is necessary to have more than one woman.

TBS IN THE FUTURE

Telephone with cord, cellular telephone, computer used exclusively to communicate on a short-term basis. There is not enough HBBs able to use the transcendental behaviors to communicate yet. On a long tem basis, the situation will be all a different matter, for not only there will be more HBBs to use the transcendental behaviors as mode of communication (, I observe that anyone I come in contact are able to use the TB, I will observe it more).—If not all—but also we may find later that regular telephone with cord and cordless telephone are harmful to our body in the long run. We may find that they cause a kind of cancer after a long period of usage. Developed used of the transcendental behaviors will be handy.

UN-USEFUL TRANSCENDENTAL BEHAVIORS

Many times when I meet a woman in the street I have the compulsion "Pelargie" or Pimbèche. Both expressions have been picked up in the street that is HBBs in my environment are thinking that way. They think that all young women are in-experimented in the love and sexual areas, whereas the less young have a large sexual apparatus. In real life things are not so. So young women started early in the domain of love and sexual experiences. It was in the news once that teenage women had already have 6 or 7 children. Nadia the Octo mum has in fact 14 children. She is not in the range of less younger ladies, but in the younger ladies category. All that is telling us that it is not question of group age but rather of individual character.

They less younger ladies are not very different in sexual apparatus dimension than the younger ladies. The less younger ones may have different emotion, having more experience in the matter for living longer than the younger ladies. After a sexual encounter the sexual apparatus of all women collapses to itself, according to what I have learned. "Pelargie" is the expression of someone who is not sexually or mentally sein. In order words we came to describe misogyny. In its extreme form can be very dangerous. I am thinking of the assassination of the young women at the university of Montreal in the 80s by Lepine (epine=prick, stab). However his name seems to have something to do with the horrible crime he committed. Who wants to have those thoughts, especially on the street while crossing nice looking women? It is called un-useful TB, could also be named "Out-rightly annoying TB".

Someone one could say that I am too much in metaphysics thinking, according to which only the useful count, the ready to wear, ready to use. It is one reason why the observation of the Creator to ground its truth is not appealing, so is not done, because it may take some time to ground the truth. It is not a ready-made device.

Despite the possible objection, I still keep this part, for some of those TBs can be very annoying. Like you just get up for the day, looking at yourself in a mirror, the person in direct communication says "neg sot". Apparently it is a way to disqualify black HBBs in North America. Any way we view it, it is annoying. Like when I had an appointment at tenancy branch and I got lost a bit in the metro-town mall. I heard the annoying voice again neg sot (stupid black). I was so pist off. Then a few second later one of the children of the previous talker repeat the same words "neg sot". I told the mother that she was a bad mother, teaching stupidities to her sons. Very annoying indeed.

USEFULNESS OF TBS

There can be connivance between 2 individual in the middle of a whole group of individuals

It is already indicated above with my case with Heidi and me here in this house where we both live. We know what we think of each other alone, the others, at least 5 persons do not know we think of each other. Because Heidi and me we communicate and have love and sexual experience with each other transcendentally.

In country like Russia, United States and England the transcendental connivance is known for they solicited me for espionage.

FIRST LAYER OF INFORMATION

When Lindsay is portrayed as having all sorts of trouble in the media (in the end of July 2010 she is in jail), my first action is to find out first hand in consulting with Lindsay herself in DP or direct communication. Most of the time she told me nothing is further from the truth than what I have heard. Recently they said that Victoria was having trouble in her marriage. I was a bit worried given that she is one of the subjects of the psychokinetic telepathy research. Via a direct perception, she said to me it was not true. When they reported not so good things about Britney, in direct communication or perception, she explained to me the context in which what was reported had taken place.

Teresa is one of the renters I had. She rented from my being a bedroom for about 8 months in the house on 16th Avenue in Vancouver. She cannot talk and cannot hear. When I rented her the bedroom someone else talked to me on her behalf. However, I did not have a too big problem to communicate with her, despite her disabilities in complete level of life. In the incomplete level of life, in DPs or direct communication there was no difference at all between her and anybody else. She communicated with me as if she had never lost her speaking and hearing abilities. In that sense the transcendental behaviors became handy, very useful indeed.

INTIMACY

Of course I am not going to write about the various kinds of intimacy I had in TBs with women. I remember I published the phrase "I know you inside out" in a text in the Internet once. Later I heard the phrase in the media. In the incomplete life, there is no substance as such, so no wall, no barrier; all things interpenetrate each other. It is not just human beings who interpenetrated each other. In that sense we are in complete intimacy, even too much intimacy like when I was making love to the raw inside a woman, where I saw all her flesh hanged out, although I do not know what that supposed to mean. Really DP and TBs in general is intimacy of intimacy. We cannot get more intimate than that. Love with these behaviors is very prevalent.

A BETTER UNDERSTANDING OF EVENTS

Armed with direct communication, direct experience and direct perception, we are better off in knowing an event. Not that it would be wrongly reported in the medias, but with kind of traditional communication used is bound to be misconceived. It is more likely that the report will miss an aspect or many aspects of the event. With the interpenetration of thing as indicated above with transcendental behaviors, it is almost impossible to overlook an aspect of the event. In regard to HBBs, the person involved in the event may misunderstand it for many reasons: physical sicknesses, unconsciousness, feelings and so on. When we have the ability to use TBs we are immune to this kind incomprehension. Many times while I am solving a problem it is the voice from afar that tells me the solution. Sometimes I am even surprised that a voice from afar tells me the solution of my own problem.

BETTER UNDERSTANDING AND DURATION OF RELATIONSHIPS

When we use the transcendental behaviors in a couple we understand each other in a way that could not happen if we did not use them. We have the inner report on each other's feelings almost instantaneously, on each other agreement and disagreement. I remember that a few things occur that would affected the relation between Maria and me like when she had trouble with one of my tenants, like when I had to tell Kitty that I spent money for her. Afterward we consulted with each other in TBs and decided that nothing changed, that we were going to continue to like each other the same. We were in circumstances that were not very accommodating to talk, but we understood each other nevertheless.

This is left to be tested in the complete life realm of things, for I am not in couple situation since for a long period of time, I cannot know if a couple of which I would be one member would do well. However the women friends I have in complete life last, like Barbara, Maria. The ones I have in incomplete life last even more so. My friendship with Britney, Her majesty started in 2003, last for about 7 years. The equation is simple, most of couples split because of a lack of contact, a lack of communication. When we ad the TBs in our baggage of tools, the likely-hood for the relationships to last rises up at least hundred-fold. For we would be in contact practically all the time. Lack of contact would not be the cause of the split in a relationships.

THE CREATION OF OBJECTS

I wrote a few books already, plus the one I am writing now to speak of my creation, plus some more to come. I intend to create an Earthquake detector, a psychic register to record our dreams or DPs, this experiment on psychokinetic telepathy, another experiment on numbers, I will try to organize the Humanizing Week to celebrate our creator and ourselves, to organize the union of Africa. Obviously without the help of the transcendental behaviors, I would not be able to think that I can do those things.

The humanizing week will probably be the last week of April given that it is cooler temperature in all countries of the world that time. I want that week to be a statutory holiday in the whole world (paid holidays). I do not know yet know what is going to happen during those 7 days, for I cannot put a lot of time on it and recruit the organizers yet, because I would not be able to afford the necessary trips if I do it right now. United Nations will play a role in the organization of it probably. I have no idea yet what it is going to be. I just think that it would be appropriate for each country to send a gift to the rest of the countries of the world that week of the year. The last time I was told that there are 190 countries in the world that is to 189 gifts to send. Obviously it can be anything, even a postal card. If there were wars in some place I would like all the belligerents to stop during the 7 days.

May be the green movement would like to join, still the accentuation will be on HBB's authentic life and the Creator.

I have the African project since 1982. Apparently before I can do it I had to do other things like stopping the cold war liberate Germany and so on. Yesterday (today is Wednesday June 23 2010) I decided for it to happen soon and also to stop the Afghan war soon too. Africa has great potentials. In Haiti we say "Union fait la force". Africa will be better off united than not. I think it is not necessary for me to go there to do it however it would be more reassuring if I go there.

The project Afghan is not among my goals because it us circumstantial, nonetheless I wanted to stop this war at the end of the month of June or at the beginning of July 2010. I wanted also some kind of contract before I start to try to stop it. Some of the leaders of the countries involved are more interested in me taking care of their individual troubles than their countries'. I decided that last Tuesday June 22, 2010. If war is used to create employment. We are not out of the wood yet I just had the intuition and it is the most idiotic thing I have ever heard. It is like none of the parties want the war to stop, one afghan warrior told me "We like American" It is like the are better off if the war is there. These groups of HBBs are at war a long time ago. I remember speaking of the subject in a kind of press conference in France in 1981.

All that because I work in the field of our Creator and because of the psychokinetic telepathy research.

THE PSYCHIC THERAPY

When Britney wAs sick in hospital, I sent her flower, but I was also frantically working psychically with her to get her out of the situation. Right now I am trying to help her to quit smoking with the TBs only. The same for Lindsay, I tried to help her when they say that she is in trouble, which happened not to be true most of the time, Right now they say that she his in low point, because she does deny it in DPs or other transcendental behaviors, I am trying to help her psychically.

THE MAGICAL SOLUTION

Last night (Today is Wednesday May 12, 2010) in a DP I arrive at an entertainment place and through the windows I saw a kind of energetic activity going on It was like the servers and the bartenders were all happy. Inside I saw A man-eating food on the small table in a disorderly fashion. When I look at him he said to me it is because he likes Reality. In direct communication, I was already called Reality. I do not know yet quite what that means. Still it speaks of magical solution coming right from Reality, from the divine realm like the little letter I sent to Ottawa worrying about the future of the loony, letter which creates a new way of governing, a new wave of governments. Thus it is magic.

There is what is named the psychedelic plants, the synthetic products to induce spiritual experiences. These plants and drug can be very dangerous. Furthermore they are forbidden in most countries of the world. There is no need to use physical product to induce transcendental behaviors. After some practices with DP in sleep (we only have to reinforce them), the direct communication and perception abilities are freed. Everyone has DP in sleep. So all the 3 abilities are free to have without the use of physical products, so that is another usefulness of the TBs, no need of drug or psychedelic plants.

THE ABILITY TO COMMUNICATE TO THE DEAD

Just after the death of Ossama Ben Ladin I saw him the first time like a person but as tall as 10 floors building in a DP that I did not understand at first

Then, because that time I was still looking for him, not knowing he was already dead until he told me in a consequent DP that his body was in the rubbles. I know from that moment that he was dead I wrote a letter to the Delta Representative Member of Parliament and send it to him telling him that Ossa was definitely dead. In about a month later while watching I have Global TV I have heard Chris said that there was a rumor that he his dead.

Later when Ali Butho ex-Prime Minister Of Pakistan was dead I saw her two a bit like fist DP with Ossama, a person Upright but as tall as many sky Scraper Building. I did not talk to her, but the reminds me that when HBBs do not want to stay alive they get in touch with me only after they past away, meaning that I could keep them alive if they got in touch with me before the event.

Just after Michael Jackson past away he told me that he was frozen in a DP. Just a few days after he told me that there are things that are unbearable to him and that some days he was a star and some other days he was not. Just after the recent death of Arnold Coleman in one of my DPs he was doing some very energetic movements, after that he told me that he was killed and repeated the statement in s few other DPs. I do not believe him. Her screen brother knew him very well, explained in TV all the miseries that affected Arnold before his death. In that context I said to myself that his wife did a stupid thing to put a basket on her dead husband body to collect money, but she does seem to be a killer. So much so that it looks like Arnold Coleman has been a victim of his own last name, if we compare someone dead with someone who is cold.

After one weak or so after their death, they became silent. I belief that if we question any dead person they can communicate with us otherwise they remain silent.

I saw also Marilyn Monroe in a couple of DPs after watching a few films in which she plaid. At that period of time I was particularly attracted to blond women I did not remember What we talked about during the DP, and I do not want to back talking to her in another DP. The ability to communicate with the dead is developed while doing the research on psychokinetic telepathy. I did not real y develop the ability. It came to me in the sense that the dead persons approached me first. I did not even know if that was possible before many experience with them (such as Hitler, Stalin, Abraham Lincoln, and so on). Some of them appeared to me as images on a wall.

Ossama kept recruiting new members for the Talibans after his death, because the West did not declare him dead officially a month or so after his physical absence. I know that because while he dead he tried to recruit me too.

Despite it all, despite what has been said above, that the good sides of the transcendental behaviors outweigh the bad sides, that the TBs will become a mode of communication at the same stage than the other modes, that human beings will be able to develop most of their potentials on their own, universities and schools will be useful not only for the skills they teach, but also to transmit knowledge in order not to have to relearn, to reinvent and rediscover all the time.

Chapter 7

EFFECTS OF THE RESEARCH

I do not have a particular interest in demonstrating that the research is scientific. I would stay away from that topic, especially because I consider that psychology took the worse course of action when the mental (and the emotional) were left behind to promote the scientific attitude. Not only that gives us a psychology in "catimini" with researches confined in the superficiality of laboratory environment, but also that has prevented us from finding the solutions of our big problems, from getting close to the truth of our Creator. However speaking of science is speaking of causes and effects. This chapter is a sign that the psychokinetic telepathy research is scientific.

LIFE IN THE SAME HOUSE THAN: A-A MAN NAMED TORI

At that time I was renting bedrooms in the house I rented on 3339 W. 42 Ave. All I remember of Tori is that he did not want to pay the rent, I had to call his mother to make him pay. He was a young man of about 25 years old and tall.

It reminds us of another event in the house. There was a filmmaker who came to me one day and said that she wanted to use the house to make a film. I accepted, but I did hear of her again. Later learned that the film was shot at another house in the same bloc. I was having difficulty with the other HBBs in the same neighborhood, probably because I did not talk to them much. There were many men living in the house. I did not have girlfriend. The neighbor who had his or her house picked to make the film might have said to the filmmaker that I was a homosexual.

I think the house I was living in was picked at first because of the research in psychokinetic telepathy I started doing in that house. The filmmaker has lost the opportunity to pass to history. Still Victoria Spelling with the small name Tori was the real reason I met the man named Tory and the filmmaker.

A1-THAN A MAN NAMED CHRISTIAN

He moved in the same house at 3393 W" 42 Ave in January from Germany. At that time I was advertising in the Province. They publish the ad in the Internet too where Christian would have read it. He was going to the University of British Columbia on bicycle from the house I rented. I met him at the corner of Dunbar street and 41st Ave. I told him that I received a call for him and that it was very bad news for a joke, He look upset. However Nadine Chanz, one of the subjects for the experimentation was the real reason we met. She also is German.

A2-BARBARA BALLANTYNE

When I moved to the house at 3538 W. 16th Ave, Barbara was living there before me. I rented the basement of the house from her. She is married with Todd, they rented the whole house, sub-rented the basement to Tamara who was about to go back to England and Australia, I moved in the house in May 2000. Barbara and Todd bought a house located on 19th Avenue two steps form the old one where I was living. Barbara is a very friendly woman. I get the impression she would give me anything if she could. Todd also is a good friend. Barbara told me last week (today is Saturday April 24, 2010) that she speaks German. I know that she is of Germanic descent, her father and her mother are German, but I did not know she speaks German before she told me.

I saw the film borrowed from the library; the title is Eva, if my memory is good on that. It was by the end of the Second World War, Eva Married a man who was still fighting at the war. She slept with other men but told them that she will never marry them because she is already married. The Black American military man was killed by Eva in an altercation involving Eva, her husband and the black man. Eva went to jail for a while then, after her liberation, she met a businessman. He died and left Eva and her husband his fortune. The film may describe a small part of German woman character, for human being characterization is lot more than that a lot more complex.

Barbara moved from the upper part of the house to go to live in hers. A couple Daniel Simca and Maria his wife moved in. Daniel made a few suggestions of homosexuality, I ignored them for he has a wife may be the sweetest woman I ever meet. I noticed her love for me from the start. It never wavered until I left the place. She suggested making love with me many times. Each time I was taken by surprise, Also I was protecting myself a bit, not having been with a woman for so many years I know that my sensitivity is very high in the domain, I would fall in love very quickly with almost any woman, I would get attached, so I kept a little bit of a distance when possible. I hogged her once and touch her crutch a bit while pushing her to her widow to get in, after being locked out by her son Diego to young to be able to open the door back. I felt a great deal of emotion that day, almost incapable of keeping myself from plunging on her and make love to her. I did not do that. I do not know really why still now.

Barbara is selling a product made of an herb called Calendula. She says that it is good remedy against skin rashes.

Daniel has a mother equally very sweet. U did not make love with her either.

Maria was not hiding her feelings for me. When her husband came in the room where we were talking, she made a noise that makes the husband leave. They come from Venezuela. Maria went to Venezuela, psychically asking me to join her there. Not being able to take care of myself really, I did not want to wreck her marriage and bring her to my life in misery. They day I was about to leave the place she came near me ready to make love with me. That day I was very upset by having to move helped by kitty. She called for a whole moth offering to help me move out" I refused. The day before I moved Maria talked to me about saying that Kitty was feeling bad about me refusing to let her to help me. To please Maria I accepted.

I did not trust Kitty, they way she asked me to move out without a just cause filled my suspicion on her. Instead of moving my things in the apartment or near it she let everything in an alley. The custodian of that place in Wellington Avenue close to Kingsway asked the guy I was going to live with to move out the next month. The guy decided to move on 15 of September, 2009, Not having enough time to find another place, I was in shelter for a while. All that for listening to Maria.

At University I took courses of German and Spanish, I still want to go to Germany and Spain in order to speak these languages. Maria is half German, half Spanish. This is rather why we met. Still these descriptions are in direct link with Nadine Chanz again.

A3-ANGELA

Was living with me in the house at 3339. I did not get to know her much. She wants to make love with me. I was not quite ready to do that with her. Part of the explanation of that was I was harassed by men in the house for sexual encounter. I was a bit against sexuality then. She was born in Winnipeg of Jewish parent Like Victoria Spelling, one of the subjects of the research

A4-GHARNIA ALLEN

Is of Indian of India ancestor, why her first name is spelled like that I guess. She was a little like Penelope, a bit deranged. It is a pity for I would love to make love with her. She was the final drop in the glass to spill the water in it. She was the one who occasioned my moving out of the place I was living in for 10 years (16 the Avenue) and all the misery I encountered afterward. I got very mad at kitty, the landlord for showing herself at the place without preventing me of that. She wanted to talk to Gharnia who was not even there at the time. Apparently she loved Gharnia too; Daniel Maria's husband made pass at Gharnia too. She must be a very sexy woman without knowing it, although she had a lot of male friends, she said to me that she was not sleeping with them. She was living on welfare money at that time.

She did not pay the rent for a whole month and she did not want to move out. I sent an e-mail to Kitty in Toronto to tell her that the rent money for July, 2009 would be disturbed because Gharnia Allen did not pay and did want to move out. Instead of discussing the rent money with me, Kitty took a plane and came back to Vancouver. Invited me to meet her at a Tim Horton' cafe. There I get mad at her again, she asked to move out I told her there will be no contest. For I always thought that when the owner of the house asks you to move out it time to vacate the place without a fuss.

Above all Jennifer Allan, one of the subjects of the research is the reason I met Gharnia Allen, knowing that I have tried to be soft with her. I do not know how she exactly interpreted my softness toward her. She refused to pay the rent for 2 months and that was partly why I got evicted to the place myself.

A5-HEIDI

It was bizarre what was happening between us. The first day we talked she suggested to me to give her a bicycle. The same day we met in the laundry room I had a DP on her. It was not clear if we made love or if we were about to do it in the DP. It seems like she was making the same dream, woke up from it and meet me in the laundry room with the hope that I was going to ask her to come in my room to make love with her or in her own room to do it. I found those things out only afterward. If I knew, on the spot I would comply with her desire.

We made love a couple of times in DP later.

Then after many weeks without seeing each other a Sunday in June 2010, she met me in the laundry room. I was taken by surprise for the number of days we did not see each other. We said hi to each other, she looked at me and work away. Later I found out that she just came back from

Ontario where her parents live and that she wanted to make love with me or something similar, without any physical clue to let me know. Again, I was taken by surprise.

At the end of May we had an altercation. I asked her to give to Musa who is living on the same floor than her the rent money for me she refused squarely. Later I had the compulsion that I was treating her like a secretary what she resented fiercely. I do not even know in which room she was living upstairs. All the males in the house are homosexual and harassers. So I keep to myself. I do not know if Heidi were aware of that or not. The first day I talked to her I did not remember to ask her telephone number or her e-mail address. One of the guys who were living here had her e-mail address. I did not dare to take it from him.

The other bizarre behavior of her is that she knocked the door of everyone on the basement floor except mine. She talked to them freely for long time, but talk to me only in the laundry room very quickly. So I have no physical link with her what so ever. I came back from New York on June 17, 2010. Sunday after she came in that laundry room while I was about to cook, She said she was going to move out in two weeks. I asked her if she was going to keep in touch with me. She said she did not know. It was the last time I saw her. I thought if she was letting me know what she was doing it was because the relation was still on, but reality seems to be saying something different. No love no go.

A6-THE AMERICAN

I call him the American because I do not remember if I asked him his name or if he told me his name but I do not remember, and because he told me he is American. He told me also that he is learning to be a doctor, and that his discipline is pathology. Of course there is a part in this book called pathos that I conceived and wrote long time ago. He just moved in next to me at the beginning of this month, August 2010. It is not a coincidence that he moves in the bedroom next to mine. Probably we have been communicating in TBs since a long time ago. I said that Heidi was behaving as if we knew each other before she cane to live here, that she chose to live here because of my presence here,—She might thought that I was rich now also—and the research in psychokinetic telepathy and the transcendental behaviors It is the same case for the American too. We have been in communication through the TBS.

A7-MICHAEL GOODHART

He was living in Shelter before I sub-rented to him the other bedroom I had at 3538 W. 16th Avenue. The relation did not last long for not only he too wanted sexual encounter with me, but also he was not paying the rent and did not want to move out. I had to threat to remove him out of the bedroom myself before he left. One day I had to go to court the day after, 39.5 millions $ were at stake, he plaid a fit, I had to call the police. I did not do well in the court that time. Recently I met him on 41 Avenue in the Kerrisdale village in Vancouver; I did not recognize him he did. It was as if he knew before hand that I was going to be at the place where he was waiting for me. The time he spent at my place I gave him money almost everyday, not a lot of money but $1 0r $2. He is of Jewish decent, so that was another connection via the transcendental behaviors and Victoria Spelling. I do not know if the misery I had with him count among the reasons why Tori do not contact me.

A8-PENELOPE

A middle age HBB, half Jewish and half Spanish was quite a woman, was suffering from a mental sickness apparently (MS). Sometimes she stood near the neighbor's house and yelled the words she was speaking for about 15 to 20 minutes, Again I had to call the police to get her out of the house. She gave me a real headache. At the Tenancy branch one person asked me when I am going to learn how to evict a person, thinking that it was that easy with her and her psychosis. She too was a connection with Victoria. The bad relation with her may have affected Victoria in regard to the research.

A9-MUSA KALAORA

After many problems with homosexual HBBs and moving from one place to the other, just a week before January 2010, I move here at 923, 20th Avenue. The house is rented by Musa, he subrent many rooms in it. The situation in this house is not a lot better than the previous ones, but I have to adapt if I do not want to end up in the street again. Musa was born in Turkey. He seems to be a nice guy but may be too nice. I do not quite know yet how he fits with the research except that there was an incidence between Turkey and Israel recently.

B-LIFE IN T SAME HOUSE THAN MICHAEL LOGIE, DEREK JACKSON

They are not directly links to our subject the effect of the experiment on psychokinetic telepathy. They way I lived in the same house with the two to form the name of Michael Jackson and what happened to the singer after ward is strange, the reason why I am describing it here. To know more about it please read The Soul Exposed. He was accused of molesting children after I lived close to these 2 guys.

I got in touch with Michael many times via transcendental behaviors, a few times by writing him, obviously when he was alive mostly. I did not have the luck to meet him in person. However he married Debbie. I went out with a woman with first name Debbie for 6 years starting 1985. His son has Prince in his names like my last name. So there was connivance between us explainable only via transcendental behaviors that I discovered while doing the research in psychokinetic telepathy. Was he accused because of that connivance and the 2 guys I was living close by? I do not think we will know the answer to that question.

C-Fax From a Couple Living in Germany

Having to move so many times, it is not clear if I am going to be able to find the copy of the fax. At that time I was going to University of British Columbia. Another student named Bill translated it for me. A short letter, I do not remember what it said, but at the end they sent me lot of kisses.

The thing is how the couple living in Germany can know that I was doing the research and that I was asking these ladies including Nadine from Germany equally, to contact me to say that they know I was doing the research and that they get in touch with me for this purpose, while I received nothing from Nadine herself? It is at least a bizarre situation. There is an idea in applied philosophy that says that Reality does what we ask for, but in its own way. We can know our goals, still the way they will come to us escape us. The fax was received in 2001. The couple did exactly what I was asking Nadine to do. Another miracle of transcendental behaviors.

E-mail from Victoria Silvstedt

The e-mail is probably still at excite site. I use to visit the site frequently, less so after I was forced to view all their ads to be able to read an e-mail sent to me. Then they had thousand of ads.

This Victoria is from Sweden, the last Playmate of the year in the CDROM with that name in which is also Nadine and Jennifer. In the e-mail she said that she knows that I am keeping secret. I described here why I could not talk about the subjects to anyone in other not to compromise the result of the research. It is what Victoria Silvstedt is alluding to in her e-mail to me. Nonetheless I wrote to Victoria once asking her if she wanted to go out with me. I did not have any answer from her on time. I let it go. After a while after I started doing the research I decided that I could talk to anyone about the research if I do not talk about the subjects. I never met Victoria St, yet she had a way to communicate with me given that I wrote her once. She did not have my contact via transcendental behaviors, eves though she knew the secret as she said. The secret is the experiment in psychokinetic telepathy with the ladies. That how the transcendental behaviors Plays a role.

CALL FROM A MAN NAMED NADINE

We did not meet as such; he called me in a little mall in the area where I was living, 16th Ave. He was inquiring about a bedroom I had for rent. I was a bit surprise, because for me Nadine was the first name of woman only and heard that that was a man's voice the bedroom might have been already rented. Nonetheless, he reminds us of Nadine Chanz with whom I was doing the research in psychokinetic telepathy.

WINNING THE SOCCER CUP

Just a few weeks before they won the soccer 2010 cup, the Spanish HBBs were under a severe look by the rest of the European HBBs. because it was supposed that their economy would drag down the Euro, although on a report on TV5, the Spanish Economic Minister defended well his country economic activities in which there was no sign for panic such as in even America where some big bank and other companies were in the brink of bankruptcy according to the Minister. So winning the cup is a great opportunity for the Spanish human beings to celebrate.

Do the research in psychokinetic telepathy plaid a role in the the Spanish Winnings in the international games? Being Born in Haiti, I have some history in common with HBBs of Spanish decent. Furthermore, Maria moves in the house where I was living on 16th Avenue with her husband and one sun Diego. Maria and me we became friends, until I move out of that house. Then in transcendental behaviors I had a communication with King Carlos. A compulsion on Isabella, the Spanish Queen who helps Christopher Columbus discovered America. Before that I saw a film entitled Queen Catherine in which a Spanish man fell in love with the Swedish Queen.

The day before the win I had compulsion on Daniel, to my surprise, for Maria is the one who is rather my friend in the couple. I kept saying to myself after each compulsion on Daniel that I am staying neutral on the matter that I am not in favor of the Dutch-land, neither the Spanish-land. So when we put all that I came to describe into account, it seems that the research I was doing in telepathy is linked with the Spanish good fortune.

Saturday July 24, 2010 the woman was drowning in the in the lake. Her female friend knocked at a door to look for help. The HHBs who went to the lake and save the woman was Minister and Member of Parliament Tony Clement and his family. The minister himself is in hot water figuratively speaking according to the news in a case related to Statistics Canada. Now we can say the minister is in hot water metaphorically and literally even though this time it is for a good cause. The one him and his family saved has first name Jennifer. She just told me in direct communication that she felt "traumatized". I told her to be careful next time not to go in the water if she does not know how to swim.

I would love to be at a lake right now soaking my feet in the water or even take a swim if the water is clean. What is bizarre is that in British Columbia there are some lakes in the backcountry, which are hot in summer. They called it Hot spring Lake. The other lakes have funny name like Stump Lake, Hut Lake, Starvation Lake, Dead man's Lake, Lava Lake and so on.

Obviously I tell the story because her first name is Jennifer and the psychokinetic telepathy study, since in the study one of the subject first name is Jennifer. However I did not expect to have any transcendental communication with the Jennifer who came close to be drown in the water. When I first took the decision to write about this piece of news I said to my self that I was going to say that I do not know if there is a link between the incident and the research. As Jennifer the one involved in the incident has just talked to me in direct communication I know for sure now that there is a link between the incident and the study they did not say her last name. I do not know if the two Jennifer(s) could have the same last, pr could be the same person. It happened in Port Sidney, British Columbia.

I taught a woman named Jennifer a few years ago. After I quit working there, it was like she had a promotion. With me she was learning French, because she was working for the Canadian Government. Only a small pack of Canadian employees are interested in learning French, they may not care for any other language in English Canada. In Québec the situation is reversed. They are rather to speak French. The small pack interested in other languages is women according to my long experience in teaching French.

That one was in the news a week ago, a huge beluga came very close to a South African couple in small boat in the sea there. The fact is I am interested to know why the big fish are found dead on the beach from time to time. I do not come to a solid conclusion, for after they are found, it is always said that HBBs will know how they die after autopsy. However I have never heard the result of the autopsy. It is like nobody is really care in knowing how they died in order to correct the situation if it can be corrected. In DP I saw that one big fish was in the middle of a bush of debris thrown in the sea by human. I concluded that they might die after eating rubber, Styrofoam and other sort of un-degradable object. Some of them might be lost in the sea and decide to beach themselves. Some of the big fish might be rejected by their group and again decide to beach themselves and die.

I have many animals that are my friends in DP because I see them not one time but many times. I only see the tail of a beluga once in a while in DP. She is my psychic girlfriend sort of. I do not know if there is a link between these direct experiences and what happened in South Africa.

It is the news this week again the story of Naomi Campbell, the fashion star, the ex-president of Sierra Leone who apparently gave the Star some pieces of diamond. Naomi said she did not know who gave them to her after all she was with Nelson Mandela during his charity events. According to the news the ex-president of Sierra Leone, might have killed thousands and thousands citizens of Sierra Leone to get the diamond, so if it is true he is of a very low character. Mia Faro an activist, Nelson Mandela's friend and Naomi said that Naomi knows who gave her the diamond.

A united Africa will be better equipped to take care of this kind of misdeed in the future. Before, when the word Africa came to my mind I automatically thought of poverty and safari, because it was how the continent was portrayed in the media. I thought only the rich countries had the precious metals. I have to control my automatism and think more clearly about Africa.

Nevertheless I do not know why the fuss about that now, something that happened years ago from today Monday August 2010. I do not know why it is in the news nowadays when China, Pakistan are still battling with flood and landslide that kill thousands HBBs, when Russia is burning by forest fire, when there landslide in Pemberton British Columbia, killing many, when there are so many disastrous events affecting us living on this planet earth constantly. Those events with the misery they cause make the diamond story look like something of the past, trivial, something we may forget and move on.

The last unusual event that day happened between a dog and a deer. Before I thought the deer was the most gentle, inoffensive animal. That day they show a deer attacking and mistreating a dog seriously. The deer smashed the dog's body with its sabots. Afterward the dog could walk only clumsily and the journalist show a little deer waking behind the mommy deer, probably the reason why this time the deer was so mean to the dog.

It was one of the best times in USA history for this time they pulled their troops out of a country instead of invading one. It was last week the second of August 2010; the American Troops left Iraq. It was schedule for later, but suddenly President Obama's government decides to pull them out this month. That allowed me to write about it in this book because its writing ends practically this month of August. They

In the direct perceptions reported in this book, on Tuesday August 17, 2010, there is a DP, which says "I am asked to go fishing". On Wednesday the DP says it is like you give a fish wrap. Not knowing exactly what it was about I tiptoed in them a bit in the comprehension part. Only today August 26, 2010 I remember the DPs and make the connection.

Don't be naive about it, the DP just not foresee the event it creates it too. In that case the creation is attributable to the research in psychokinetic telepathy and to the subjects-Jennifer, Nadine and Victoria. It started in 1997; the fish creation may have started since that year or any time between 1997 and 2010.

The scientist man says that they too cannot explain what happened, there are so many fish, that we have to be cautious about it. Still the reader of this book will more or less understand.

Australia, last week has elected a minority government following the trend I practically and inadvertently started in Canada by sending a letter to Prime Minister Paul Martin about the Liberal, the conservative and New Democratic party, The Canadian HBBs should have red the idea from my psyche and applied it, Canadian as well as, the Australian the English, and the French, one more time thanks to the telepathic research.

Chapter 8

EFFECT-1

HBBs Suspected of Benefiting from the Research

Who knows how many it could be? I have the impression that I animate the capacity of the transcendental behaviors in everyone I come in contact with, this capacity may be awaken in all the inhabitants of the planet by the study on psychokinetic telepathy. In that case it seems we have a New World and that New World is forever. It seems that the individual living on the planet will not be able to think that he is alone, rather will have a sense that he is connected with the rest of the inhabitants of the planet. I could name the presidents I help, the prime ministers I help, the simple individual in the street, the mute person I help, the list could go on and on. "I" here is not my ego but the imaginative "I", the one that is the resultant of individual and the world soul.

Money that would come to me. Went to Rogers Nelson

I check his previous year declared salary, it was 56 millions $ and something. I calculate that it is around the amount of money he would be earning in those days. Instead of that in 2005 he earned 84 millions $, in 2006, 92 millions $. He won Oscar Grammy etc. The fact is the surge in popularity and salary is because of the research in psychokinetic telepathy. I was mistaken for him at Hollywood. After I started the court action against him to have 39.5 millions $ from these 2 years salary, we met many times in psyche or via transcendental behaviors. He offered me homosexuality, food. One time or in one of these experiences we fought. Sometimes he had a vexing attitude.

He had this extra-fame and extra millions of $, from the research in psychokinetic telepathy and since we wear the same name Prince. In 2000 he changed his name and was called Prince the singer or something similar. The last name Prince is one he gets himself probably when he became a popular singer. The last name is the one I got since I was born, the one all my family get. In one direct communication he talked to me about Nadine who apparently has called him. Apparently I was mistaken for him at Hollywood.

He did not show up at a court hearing. When I was going to the court to find him guilty in a direct communication on the street he told me he was not going to be able to go. Afterward I found that he was going to live to Hollywood to justify his new fame and the surge in money. He made joke about me in Saturday Night Live, that I was someone who whispers in the ears of other HBBs including himself. At that time Britney and Janet Jackson and other stars talked about Prince on TV. My psychic relation with Britney started effectively in 2003 when I sent a letter to her to collect fund for the earthquake detector project and a poem, which was in fact a love declaration.

So the folk at Hollywood thought that the hoopla was about Prince Rogers Nelson.

Some times we cannot prevent ourselves from having negative feelings about someone. It was my first time in court. I asked the judge to find him guilty for no show up; the judge asked me who Judy was". Judy was Prince Rogers Nelson's spoke person. I did believe that the judge has the file in front of him that it was his duty to read it. A long time afterward I thought that they have a lot of paper in front of them, that it is the duty of the lawyer to navigate them in the files. The judge told me that the law of British Columbia does not allow him to judge to find Prince Rogers Nelson guilty for no show up. Imagine 39.5 millions at stake, they other party does not show (He move to Hollywood to justify himself). Imagine the judge telling me that the law does not allow him to find him guilty for no show up. One of the Chiapas would take a machete and go there and cut his head off.

Later I tiptoed in the court not knowing really what I was doing there, and hesitating to bring the argument of transcendental behaviors in front of the court. I had a big sense of inferiority (still a bit), I was afraid that they would see me as being insane if I talked about DPs DC and DE. Then I did not want at all to talk about the on going experiment telepathy (one of the reasons of the fame and money) in order not jeopardize the result, hoping Jennifer, Nadine and Victoria Spelling would still contact me

The Law Society of British Columbia helped me a bit I thank them for that. Still after I started to get some progress in the court, at the law society they became furious at me for that and cut the help. The tribunal accepts "indigency" fees for futilities, nothing like 39.5 millions of $. We are not out of the wood yet. I feel that British Columbia owes me the 39.5 million $.

Jennifer Anison, Jennifer Hudson, Jennifer Lopez, Jennifer Love-Hewitt

The research started in 1997, I do not know exactly when these ladies started their career, although they have great success during the time I am doing the psychokinetic telepathy study in which Jennifer Allan is one of the subjects. I am not conscious of either of the four in my psyche. Nothing is really a coincidence.

Jennifer Anison

I watched the show called Friends in which she was playing a lot. Afterward I saw her in many films. So I am a fan of heirs. I think being a fan and the telepathic research are what may have a positive consequence on her career. She is on top of her game now by being in so many films, fortunately. Her actors and actresses companions Friends may have decided not to pursue the cinema field. It is clear that Jennifer Anison has a lot of footage in the media scene than them what goes in favor of the theory, which connect the study of telepathy, Jennifer Allan and Jennifer Anison. In the research there is also Tory spelling as subject, Tory I see very often on TV? I do not have that opportunity with Jennifer Allan. The other Jennifer on TV may be a way for me to see her.

Jennifer Hudson

I do not have the knowing awareness of Jennifer Hudson in my DPs either. The psychokinetic research and the fact that we are both of black color may have contributed to the high standing she has in her acting career presently. I am a fan of her too.

Jennifer Lopez

I like Jennifer Lopez in the film called Zoro. I thought she had a nice face and a nice body before she got involved with PDD and got married. That and the research might have open the gate to some psychic experience with her that I am not aware of and that may have a positive effect on her career. If it is, so much the better.

Jennifer Love-Hewitt

She is tHe one who demonstrates the point I am trying make in this part of the book the clearest way, that Jennifer Allan, one of the subjects in the study on telepathy played a role in the career of many HBBs wearing the same first name, for the title of the series in which Jennifer Love Hewitt played is called Ghost Whisperer. I saw the series just a couple of times for a few minutes. It was like someone who was dead, some how was whispering in Jennifer's hears, was guiding and protecting her somehow. You remember that Prince the singer plaid in a sequence at Saturday Night Live a character who said that I was whispering in his hears, not that they saw me as a ghost but as a person with the ability to whisper in someone else's hears via transcendental behaviors.

The person whispering in the Jennifer's hears may not be a dead person, may be as alive as you can get. I mean the person may as well be me who am writing this book. The writer of the show or Jennifer may know that the whisperer is living body at another part of the world. However their ego may not accept that unusual situation, it may be hidden to them. Many times in DP I saw situations which are blocked from my consciousness at first, not because of anything else but the fact that what I saw is an unusual event. So we have another explanation as to why the beautiful subjects of the psychokinetic experimentation do not contact me. It is not because they do not know my contacts. Jennifer Allan suggested in a direct communication while I was doing a telepathic reinforcement session that she knows my address and all sorts of information on me. Then it is ok to conclude that she does not call because the way she gets the information on me is too unusual.

Britney, not only knows all information's about me in the second details, but also about all my family, my ancestors although she may be unconscious of that knowledge in her. The person was bugging me or was sexually harassing me. In front of the door of my bedroom I punch him in the face. Police came afterward he told them that he lost a ring that may be in my room. Years before I was going to propose to a woman, bought a gold ring; An HBB named Pancho stole the ring from me. So the harasser knew things that happened to me years ago. Now he was not my friend as such. The subjects of the experiment became my friends after so many years of thinking about them almost everyday. They know a lot more about me than my addresses, my telephone numbers and my e-mails addresses. In life and death apparently HBBs know a lot more about each other then they think.

Who knows how many HBBs living around Jennifer, Nadine and Victoria, or in the same city than them, or in the same country than them who are benefiting from the research?

WHERE THE RESEARCH HAS NO INFLUENCE

After noticing that a number of Canadian soldiers in Afghanistan are dead just before they are about to get free and come back home, I have sent a number of letters to the Canadian troops there telling about my observation. I told them that those deaths are avoidable and that should be by keeping the soldier in office a few days before they are due to go. Yesterday I learned that one guy of 24 years were killed by a bomb. He was 2 days due to leave. The military there do not seem to care about such idea. So the research fails in that sense.

I sent letters to Ottawa (Wednesday, February 3, 2010 and to Washington (Wednesday November 25,2009) offering my help to stop the war in Afghanistan if they sent me a contract saying that they will pay me a certain amount of money after the end of the war. I have no answer of both governments Today Monday May 17, 2010. These words were also published in the Internet. I have just had a compulsion on "certificate", it made me laugh, given that there no institution able to give me a paper for this ability, for it does not exist any where else, but in my dwelling with the psyche, no one else is capable of accomplishing such a thing like stopping a war. Washington and Ottawa, Americans and Canadians are certainly interested in stopping the war. I do not know why I am not hired to do it. Psychokinetic telepathy research has no influence on them, on this part of the political arena that is clear.

THE WAY IN WHICH THE RESEARCH INFLUENCES AND WILL INFLUENCE THE PUBLIC ARENA

I notice that the bank where I have an account for about 18 years merges and become TD Canada Trust. There they are more clientele oriented now, In the brochure I take from the bank, there is an effort to make their clientele more comfortable in dealing with them. It seems to me I have a profound impact on the HBBs where I lived and am living now. After not seeing them for about 6 months, when I saw them recently I was surprised to find that Todd, Barbara's husband is working inside of their house, doing a consulting work. I lived in the same house than them during 6 years and I was always working inside the house from 7 to 5 five days a week. I did the errands in the after 5 PM and during the weekend. I felt so responsible when I learned that, hoping I do not draw them in making error by my style of life. I did suggested to them to by a house with the money they were paying for rent. They seem to be happy to have done that.

At time I feel that I have a positive influence on the whole world by doing the study in psychokinetic telepathy. At other time I feel as if I govern the whole world with an immense sense of responsibility after realizing that I could bring it the in the hole by inadvertence.

EFFECT-1

Number of Television Series Inspired by the Research

How I Met Your Mother

It was pubLished in the Site www.psychicfacultyandresearch.com in the year 2009. When Britney was having health difficulty, which necessitated that they brought her to hospital, I became mashed potato emotionally speaking. In DP I visited her house that day that I found there was her mother. She was in position to make love with me. I did hesitate a bit, a bit conscious of what was happening; however it did occur. Later Britney was furious against her mother in complete life, told the tabloid that her mother took advantage of her absence and slept with her husband. She fired her mother as director of her business and that may have cost her millions of $ stolen from her (I am sorry for that my dear), before her Father took over the business.

Who knows why we do what we do it is like that, it happened. She may have done that by jealousy, to attract my attention on the fact that there is a big chronological gap between Britney and me or simply because she was aware of that kind of psychic activity and wanted to experience it too or, according to Power of Empathy "Envy parents come to feel vis-à-vis burgeoning sexuality, eroticism and love they witness in their own off-springs".

In the tabloid they accused Britney of making her ex-husband Kevin live in the basement. It is me who was living the basement at 16th Avenue; I am still living in the basement at 20th Avenue, end of April 2010. So in the tabloid they thought that Britney's husband at that time was I, Britney was feeding the myth too by what she said to them. We are together only in direct perception, communication and experience, we never met in complete life. All in all that how the TV series "How I met Your Mother was born", because of the research on psychokinetic telepathy and the discovery of the transcendental behaviors

Deal Or no Deal

It is mentioned in a book called "Psychokinetic Phenomena". I still have the deck of card I used to exercise my intuition. I picked a card face down and guessed what it am before I put the face up. Who ever created the show changed the deck of card in many women 25 I guess (my psychic age is 25), then he had or created the show Deal or no Deal. Harry Mendrel who animated the show is Canadian as I am. Part of the show was done in Canada. The creator of the Show had a hint that the person who was doing the study on psychokinetic telepathy from which he got the idea from is Canadian. However transcendental behaviors have no boundary? What he would do best was to send me some of the money he was making with the show, which had a real impact in TV history.

The deck of cards reminds us of the tarot cards, in human psyche from a long time ago from the Roman and the Egyptian HBBs. Now and apparently they are used to predict the future. The picture on the tarot cards are made with hand drawing. Despite the great mystery and secrecy around their meanings, I think they are the start of alphabetization, the start of literature and mathematics, the start of letters and numbers, in other words the start of civilization. When I was playing or exercising my intuitive ability with the red deck of cards I still have, I did not even hear of the tarot cards.

SURVIVOR

It is only later after the show Had started I realized that Brunet the creator was part of my psychic world. Who knows how many shows he got like that" Who knows how many shows are inspired by the research in psychokinetic telepathy. At that time I was s bit oblivious to myself, did not realized the scope of the psyche, of the transcendental behaviors, the impact on the whole world, I said it before it is as if it awakes in all inhabitants of the planet the capacity to use the transcendental behaviors. James was one participant of two shows. The first show he did not win the million $, but they gave him $50 000, James is black as I am. I saw Jeff in a DP once. He asked me to be one of the participants. Thinking that I did in complete life most everything that happened during the taping of the show when I was in Haiti, knowing that I am not really "socializer", important element to win in the game. I declined Jeff's offer. Nonetheless most of the above says that Jeff and Brunet are conscious of the study as the first hand inspirer of their Survivor.

THE APPRENTICE

A bit like above, still this one draws more on that I was teaching in a School and that I was let go, in other words, it is still inspired by the research I am doing with Jennifer Nadine And Victoria as the subjects. I told the story completely in the Soul Exposed. Someone else might have told them a story to that he was the inspirer of the idea and might have got money for that, may be he was saying the truth as he knew it may be not. According to me that was a complete lie For he might have been in my part of the psyche at the same time that others while I was doing psychokinetic telepathy exercise with the subjects above. In the deep down the idea of the Apprentice transformed came from the research. This time the exploited the teacher part of me.

THE DARK ANGEL AND JESSICA ALBA

I of am dark color, I am aware of her existence in the film or televised series of recent years. I was a real admirer of her. They say she was filming in Vancouver and was staying at a hotel. I went out to try to meet; I could not find the hotel, "maladroit". When I was watching the series, I did not make any connection between the Dark Angel and the study of psychokinetic telepathy. That is to say that I did not have many DPs on her and being conscious of them and her, meaning, we can have many DPs on someone without being conscious of them and the person, in other words we block the DPs for one reason or another.

I did not talk to any of the big number of ladies in complete life yet. So I do not know how the really perceive me. In one DP once I saw myself walking like a toy beside a woman, like an hologram, myself in miniature, so I have some insight on the situation, but not in complete life. Because I did not want talk to anyone about Jennifer, Nadine and Victoria before they contact me in CL, other HBBs may think or feel that they should not talk to me about them and me in previous DPs in complete life. Above is to say that others may see me in their DPs as an angel as the title of the series Dark Angel and other televised series. It is an event, thanks to the psychokinetic and telepathic studies. She won OscarI saw her in DP a couple of times afterward), I do not know how many, still I know she won at least one. She did it of her own by the way she plaid her characters and above all by her sense of self, her perseverance. Her Oscars are heirs, not someone else's.

Furthermore the title of the series and the research remind us of characterization work on our Creator is obscure and unclear. The Soul Exposed Has many DP in it and I describe how each one is tight to the complete life, I hope the book is going to dissuade the metaphysics thinkers in their belief that dealing with "be-ing historical thinking" is not an obscure neither an unclear work True, I have most of my DPs in complete darkness, it because in those DPs, I am in the whole existence. Some HBBs like the darkness as says Ulrika Ericsson in the video in which are Jennifer and Nadine. The love of the darkness does not render observation on Reality obscure or unclear,

There are 2 other Angels in the video One is name Angel Boris; the other is Kelly Monaco of Pennsylvania. In her sequence She walks with two big bird wings of white color, which make her look like an angel. Angel is how the Creator is was perceived in the past and one too, but no one consciously made the connection between the two before me and the research on telepathy.

SCARY MOVIE 11

I think I saw the creator of this film on TV and that he is black. It is not for nothing he gave Victoria Spelling a big part in this film and I wonder if he is really conscious or if he has the knowing awareness of that I am doing a the research in psychokinetic telepathy and that Victoria is one of the subjects. There are some years since I saw the film, I remember very little of it. I remember though there is a character plaid by a man in the in the story. The character is kind of a handicap, with a hand with fingers like spider legs. It looks like it was playing me, still in a very bad light. I probably have already told the story in the Soul Exposed. The fingers make me think of my DP writing. I am barely awake when I wake up to write the direct perceptions, so the letters look like spider legs. In the film Victoria plays a part which is like a signature of the research, she plaid with the telephone I used to play with when I was a child in Haiti, that is to say, two carton cups link with a cord that can be made with sewing material or basket material, no electricity, nothing, just the cord, the cups in which two individuals are communicating with each other or are trying to communicate with each other.

One can interpret the sequence in many ways; my way is that it is saying that the telephone as we know it is something of the past. I would not say it quite like that myself, but close. For the research shows that we can communicate more effectively by using the transcendental behaviors.

However there is something they women I met in DP are doing in complete life, that I suspect Victoria also is doing that I do not quite agree with. They tend to think that if we have the transcendental behavior with which to communicate why bother using the telephone. The transcendental behaviors happen in incomplete life. The name says it well these experiences are not complete. They need that part of complete life to become complete themselves.

Victoria, Nadine and Jennifer do not seem to see things that way, they reason they would not call me in the complete life. Britney, Lindsay, Avril, Poppy, Milla, do not see thing that way, the reason why they would not contact me in complete life, no need of paper, of telephone, of fax, of e-mail, because we have transcendental behaviors. Some of their friends make me feel like I am the worse materialist in the world, a materialist exclusive, for wanting to connect the incomplete life to the complete life, for wanting them to contact me with pen and papers. They themselves are living in the exclusive spiritualism, nothing but the spiritual life. It is an exaggeration in both sides.

The ladies want me to just pack my bags and go and join them in California without any prior contact in the CL. They insist on that in this day and age of terror possibility. They stars with millions fans looking at them like mentor, as models to follow in order to succeed like them. If I just meet them that way, their fans may try to do the same and get themselves in big trouble. The stars have bodyguard. They are able to meet HBBs in psyche and meet them in complete life just like that. Their fans do not have bodyguard. They would take a big risk to behave with such an off-handed manner.

According to me the traditional ways of communication will stay. I do not want to adopt any false scientific attitude, we need verification. Yes the experience we have in the incomplete is true, essential, but it is not a complete truth. At least it is not totally comparable with the complete life situation. We cannot have a child by making love with someone in the incomplete life, despite the story of Immaculate Conception (the Creator is immaculate), despite the link between the CL and the IL, despite the usefulness of the incomplete life above. If it was I would have thousand kids by now, after so many years of making love in the incomplete life.

Yes, the incomplete life lasts forever, an attraction may be for some of us, if you want eternity, here you have it.

CHARMED

In which plaid Shannon Doherty, Alicia Milano by Aaron Spelling.

It was a televised series that I watched couple of times. I know it was an effect of the research in psychokinetic telepathy, because it was created By Aaron Spelling, Victoria Spelling's father, Victoria is one of the subject of the research. Then in the series there were 3 ladies playing the main characters, comparable to 3 ladies in the study, Victoria, Jennifer and Nadine. There were many supernatural sequences in the series, so it probably about the supernatural, individual able to have unusual experiences. Nevertheless, these experiences which are possible in DP, in incomplete life are not possible in complete life yet. One more reason to think that Aaron draws the material for this series directly from the research in telepathy where the transcendental behaviors are discovered. It is like he was in narrow connection with me for this series.

The little scale described earlier on creation explains a bit what the supernatural is, because nature is placed after the gods, the gods and goddesses are placed after nothingness, nothingness is placed after the creator (called also Reality or Universal Self). The individual soul and the spirit are in the rank of the gods and goddess (my version of creation)

SOMETHING LIKE THAT

Was The title of a movie in which plaid Angelina Jolly. I had just seen her for the first time playing in a film with Whoopy Goldberg. I had a crush on her. Later in complete life, the crush is faded, however it opened the gate of transcendental behaviors between her and me, how she or her producer, or the creator of the film might have the part of a sentence "something like hat". In DP most of the times the information I have is blurred. As said Scary Movie 11, often I can barely read what I wrote on paper immediately after I have a DP anyway. Let's say in DP I have this information: "I want you to get closer to me". When I record the DP during the day most of the time I add to the information "or something like" meaning that I did not get the information on a clear solid ground.

Although I use one film and many TV series to illustrate that the research on psychokinetic telepathy has effect on the society in many ways, although the transcendental behaviors discovered while doing the research dwell in the Reality or our Creator's field, the so called reality shows on TV are not to be confused with the Realty. They 2 concepts are almost totally different. In the reality shows they portray rather some aspects of nature. In Survivor, most of the show happens in the middle of a forest, The participants have to do what ever they can to survive the roughness of nature. In the Apprentice the would be businessmen and women are given task to try in the real business world like creating a product and sell it. So these learners are being put on the rough world of business to learn the profession. All that I came to describe are natural events, but not our Creator who create everything that exist that we know and probably many more things that we do not know.

As we saw earlier the zeal, the excitement for nature, the HBBs who are taking advantage of the situation to commercialize nature, all that will not necessarily make us observe Reality in other to ground its truth and that way keep us away from becoming mashed potato. The zeal for nature while staying away from the Creator is more likely to make of us exclusive marerialist.

WITHOUT A TRACE

I know that the concept may come alive by the number of HBBs who disappeared leaving no trace and their families in misery, still the person who plays Samantha character was a psychic friend. I even wrote her a letter and sent it to her, which she did not answer although we were together in psyche often. So the research in psychokinetic telepathy may have an influence in conceptualizing this TV series too. At that time I was worried of dying without leaving a child, anything else. I would be dying then without a trace. Poppy has a child so much the better for the child and for her. I was very displeased when I learned she was pregnant. Britney (there might have been a psychic fight between her and Britney, the same as Britney did with Natalie Glebova) had 2 children, it is like a lot of young ladies were following her steps even if it could be detrimental door them to have children "à l'impromptu". Poppy may have been worried of not having children also. During that period of time I was very miserable for all sorts of reasons, including women who attracted me and whom I could not touch physically.

"SOMETHING LIKE THAT"

I started to talk to Angelina Jolly in a psychic encounter. Somehow I name her companion Brad or I say the name Brad, Brad woke up and said "you wake me up". The same thing happened with Queen E and Prince Philip. I stated to have a communication with her majesty (she told me once to call her like that), I named Prince Philip. He woke up and started a conversation with me talking about body ach.

However "something like" is something I said a lot in the Soul Exposed, because it is made basically with DP and very often they are not very clear to me. So, according to what is said above, we may assume that the title of the film in which Angelina Jolly plaid the main character is inspired not by me but by the research in psychokinetic telepathy.

Chapter 9

EFFECT-2

Political and Other Contributions—A New Way of Governing

AUSTRALIA

This country is in a precarious situation with the recent minority government they elected. The governing group has only 2 members more than the opposition. In the world view they were saying that if someone is sick, another has to go for an unplanned trip the government would not be defeated, but the two parties with the most votes would be in a deadlock, very difficult situation indeed. I think they will have to be inventive to be able to govern without too many elections, not very good for the economy of the country in more than one way. One purpose of the minority government is good administration without having to go poll to many times I guess.

CANADA

A-C would do better C-A

At the Canada Election Day in 2004, I was a bit sad to find that Mr. Paul Martin was elected Prime Minister of the country with a minority government. I was thinking of the Canadian $ which was very week in comparison to the American $. So I sent a letter to Ottawa to calm the situation down, in order not to create political mayhem and took that way the Canadian $ even further down. In the letter I addressed each elected party chief, telling each that his own party is

98

the only one which has good ideas. I did not address Mr. Ducepe, but the letter itself was written in French.

Yes before the letter I had a DP on one Parliament Session that I did not quite understand at the time. The fact is since then there was a bit of a turmoil in the political arena in Canada last year which ended up with the prorogation of the parliament, however it did not have much an impact on the Canadian economy. The $ is a bit higher now than it was in 2004. The idea may look like a wacky idea now that the conservative party in Canada is practically governing with the democratic party, though it is, the liberal and rhea conservative have almost the same of vote un the parliament it is functioning.

It will take time before the rest of the governed HBBs get use to this new type of government. I have heard some criticism as to 1) members of the party in power become bully, are bullying the members of the other parties as if they were school children. as to 2) the parliament itself becomes ineffective, unable to the job they are supposed to be doing, meaning creating laws to make Canadian life more authentic. In regard to the first criticism, It is possible to imagine that some members of parliament feel that they do not have to be too precautious toward their colleagues, that they have a solid deal with a party to kept them in power, that there is no fear of falling off by inadvertence and by being disrespectful toward a parliamentarians. It is a new way of governing. Excesses will made in both sides of the political continuum before their could be and adjustment in the middle.

The second criticism is also related to the new phenomenon (needs time to fully unravel) in governing. The Canadians who are not parliamentarians are still expecting "the draw of the sword" (this is a metaphor, still in certain countries it occurs in complete life once in a while) type of working parliament. If it is not that way it is supposed to be ineffective, despite that the Canadian economy seems to be improving, in good time which would be the real criteria for knowing if a parliament sessions are effective or not.

Then there is Michael Jean, born in Haiti like myself, governor of Canada. Did I help her getting that position? I did not know her existence before the job. So it hard to say. Although there was great psychic friendships between and ex-Canadian Prime Minister Paul Martin and me. Michael Jean was chosen as governor of Canada on his mandate.

There is a cap put on the Canadian economy by the Canadian themselves. I observed that in the lottery game Called Max. The first prize reached 50 millions $ since last month June 2010. Than the game directors decide that they will not let it go further like in State where it went up to 300 millions, like Spain where they let it for up 800 millions $. They directors of the game would argue that they want to spread the to more Canadians by having a number of one million prizes at the same time. May be true but it is a cap on how much one person can win anyway.

I am not saying that it is very bad, but it tastes a bit like Marxism or other kind of dictatorial government.

EFFECT-3

Olympic Game: Helping Canada Win Gold Medal

I was not quite interested in the Olympic game. As I describe it above, I have already many things in my plates of creation; many of them are still in future tense. They necessitate money that I do not have yet to create them. So I have little time left to be preoccupied by the winter Olympic game in February 2010. However, other part of me did not see it that way, or I was psychically coerced by Canadians to take care of them regarding the gold medals. For in a DP I saw myself walking side by side with a little group of HBBs. Beside me there was one who very tall one. After I woke up I was wandering who she could be. When Christina Nesbit won the gold medal in rapid skating, I realized that she was the person beside me in the DP. She might have been in my DPs before; still it was the first time I was aware of it. We started to have direct communication since then. Like when I have just started to write this paragraph she said to me "I am your friend". Then the Canadian team kept winning medals with many gold medals for the first time in Canadian Olympic game history.

There is also Joanie Frechette with whom I am in direct communication. I hope I could marry her. There is also Ksenia of Russia Makarova who won a gold medal during Winter Olympic game 2010 and who communicate with me a few times via the transcendental behaviors, and so on.

Who knows what Gérard de Coubertin had in mind when he created the Olympic Games, may be it was a humanitarian idea to get the world together once in a while to create other occasion of meeting than war. War still continues to happen. In the Worldview I heard the talk of 3rd World War, that, according to the speakers, had started with the 9/11 event. So we are even close to war instead of getting away from it. So the humanitarian goodwill in the Olympic Games is not working so well. The idea seems to be lost in capitalist gambling, so much so that there is ranking in the game: first, second, third prize or gold, medal, bronze, what is the 3rd? Platinum? The ranking could reinforce, self-amelioration, self-transcendence. The pervasive results in the world seem to indicate that it reinforces rather the ego culture. We are not out of the wood yet.

Later, someone else may say the same about my idea of Humanizing Week that I intend to start at about the last week of April.

ENGLAND

The letter seem to have a positive influence in politics, especially on governing in Canada, and in some other countries in the world. For in England, the same governing pattern seems to be adopted, since, yesterday (Today is Monday May 10, 2010), the English electors chose to give no party a definite mandate. Sooner or later, there will be a coalition of parties governing the England (It is actually the Conservative and the liberal parties). Yes the electorate may have been inspired by the Obama (agenda from my ideas too) movement, still they have the situation in Canada to tell them that there is not much to fear of coalition government.

FRANCE

The political situation has changed if France Also. Nicolas Sarcosi is France citizen, still the name Sarcosi may be of a different ancestor then French. Anyway, the French electorate seems to be pursuing a different kind of politics by electing Mr. Sarcosi as their President, a bit the same situation in United State. I met the couple Sarcosi in DPs and feel like friend toward them. I do not know if there is a connection between the research and the election of President Sarcosi. I do know a Canadian traveled all the way to France to save a French previous President, living in the same city as myself, working in the same school I worked before. There is certainly some Psychokinetic telepathy in it,

GERMANY

That spontaneous help has happened years ago, still it is important to remind ourselves of it again. The liberation of Germany is something I helped doing with love. with the help of the research which only in my psyche at that time. Because in "real" life it would be strange to say that we stop war with love. It sounds banal to me too, though it happened by loving Raya and Angelika in Winnipeg. I do not know if the name Raya has a specific sense in Russia, Angelika (the name suggests the Creator also) certainly suggest an angel, the way I could be called because of my dwelling in TBs.

To Name a Few.

RUSSIA

I do not do active politics, never voted for a party in my whole life. It is an irony that I can talk like this about politics today, although I resented that Pavlov did not submit any psychological point of view in politics at his time when his inspiration was badly needed, would be so useful for Russia and the rest of the world, what would spare the world of a lot of headaches. I helped the country to come back to itself and continue helping the rest of the world with its ingenuity and his great thinkers, as it was around the time of Pavlov.

UNITED STATES OF AMERICA

Wanting to make money to make ends meet and to materialize other projects (was published in the internet this year) I was looking for Ossama Ben Laden, nevertheless, in my psychic exercises, I was told that his body was in a Barack in Afghanistan, many times. Of course then I did not know if somebody was wearing the name Barack, neither if he could be President of United States. When I found that out I resented it a bit thinking that he was blocking my vision during the search. Now I think it was for a bigger cause, may be.

OTHER CONTRIBUTIONS

THE HARRY POTTER AND THE TWILIGHT SAGA

I used to play the lottery game; there was a set I called rouge cruche for red pot in English. JK Rowling was a teacher like I was. So there are some commons points between us. Although nowadays there is a demand for story like Harry Potter and the Twilight Zone, for the supernatural phenomena one may supposed that I am behind those two or the research is behind them. It looks like there is the thirst for the supernatural, however it is not clear if the hunger is also for spiritual life and for the Creator, two of the main reasons I do the study. By now it is clear for all of you that via the transcendental behaviors any one gets information from anyone (any one from any one may be not now, anyone from me, certainly in the future). The Harry Potter series would be behind the Twilight Saga, Psychokinetic telepathy behind Harry Potter, although my book is not yet published. They give parties in the basement. I am still living in the basement. In TV reporter repeated many times that she does not know why the obsession with the Twilight phenomenon. This is part of the answer.

This afternoon (now it is ten pm) I was reflecting upon it and asked myself why they are making billion dollars of the idea,

While the first version of this book was rotting in drawers so much so that I lost it, while I am still living in a kind of poverty?

I do not have the answer of the question.

It was the Canada Day or Birthday; I took a bit of a break so I could watch the Oprah Show. She invited three actors and actresses . . . on her show. I saw 2 men actors at the David Letterman show later. The night before I had a DP that I thought was about Briny. I was with her outside her house with her children; She entered into the house with her kids and closed the door leaving outside while saying that I am a stranger. In this twilight zone there is a similar sequence. So the DP was about Oprah Show, the Twilight phenomenon, and Britney.

I already mentioned that around the arrival of the G29 in Toronto, there was a bit of natural turmoil in that part of Canada, specially a twister in Saskatchewan and an earthquake of magnitude 5 felt in Toronto, Ottawa. to the explanation I previously wrote in this book I have to add that in New York recently one of my brothers told me that another brother has a son somewhere in the Prairies, recently immigrated there. So the natural turn-moil in that region of Canada was not just a warning to me of the G 20 visit there, but also to attract my attention to the nephew I have living there. Yes, to attract my attention nature sent a twister and an earthquake, although nobody was dead in the events. Imagine, The Creator, the universe, or simply the nature is talking to me by creating a twister and an earthquake, just as some of my psychic friends talk to me via TV, meaning they create an event in TV to send me a message when they do not use one of the transcendental behaviors. It is something.

In 2003 I contacted many HBBs asking for research grants. about a dozen. J.K. Rowling was the only one who answered me, even though it did not go further because I did not quite understand her answer. She did a great work with the Harry Potter Saga, I congatulate her for the wonderful books and films she wrote with her idea

MADONNA'S BLACK PRIEST SONG

I saw her in a couple of DPs I visited her place in DP and we have some direct communications. In one DP recently she said to me "I am your object", I was surprised. When she was about to adopt her boy and they were making a fuss I said to myself she should adopt me instead. When I was still teaching I listened to her music a lot. I saw a couple of films in which she plaid. I am a fan.

In the song the word "whisper" would be the link with me and the research in telepathy. For in a sequence in Saturday Night Live Prince the singer had already alluded to the whispering as if it is the way I am perceived in direct communication. When I heard the song it was as if it was speaking to me directly,

BUSINESS CONTRIBUTION

Prince the singer was earning around 50 millions $ a year, thanks to the research in psychokinetic telepathy especially trough the transcendental behaviors, his salary picked dramatically to 84 and 92 millions $ in a relatively short period of time in early 2000 years. It is these kinds of business I am thinking of.

Similar to such a positive event in regard to Fido, the cellular phone company and the research. The place that I rented 1995, and sub-rented was sold in December 1999. So I did not Have a stable living space for a while neither a stable telephone. It is this context I became a fido customer in 2000. At that time the company was scarcely known, scarcely visible. After a year or so using their phone company became a billionaire company or with an asset of a billion $. The company central office is in Montreal where I live for 6 years before moving to Manitoba and British Columbia. This factor counted in me buying their service, so in making them a billionaire company. The research in telepathy is the culprit of all that. Why not me?

Prince the singer and the windfall million $ that would come to me but were deviated to him and Fido are only 2 examples of business contribution, there are a lot more, if we count the number of services one individual needs in order to live. Cloth Company, shoe company, Soap Company, tooth brush and tooth paste companies, food company, entertainment company. Book stores, and the list can be even longer. In other words all these companies benefit too some how.

BUSINESS FOUNDATION

Since 1991 after I was let down from the last school where I was like a teacher on call I became self-employed. I worked in the housing industry a bit at government election a bit. All the time I was doing the research in order to be able to create my goals. The business was called Supra-conscience at a time. The name evolved into Psychic Faculty and Research. About 4 years ago I created a site www.psychicfacultyandresearch.com. I noticed that the owner of the mother site Fortune City now Dotster was selling the name by adding. ca.org, all in all by adding a slight modification. The name of the company is not registered yet. That is another Story. The real story here is while reading Heidegger's book Mindfulness at the end of 2009 I noted the following phrases with arrangement" HBBs could find his her way at the site of decision of his swaying attunement of be-ing." It is as if the site I created a few years ago was foreseen by him long time ago and that the decision to create the site was in me since I was born. A bit bizarre. In the site I write about the Creator often.

MOST EUROPE A "GYLANY"

That part of European heritage hidden under the hoopla of modernity is not a contribution of the research, although I would not know about it if I did not do the research on psychokinetic telepathy. According to a Lithuanian Anthropologist Majia Gimbutas has red a book written in 1861 by a Swiss jurist "Mother'Rights". According to Gimbutas Most Europe was a "gylany" same rights for both sexes at a certain point in time. Yes that was the political way of most Europe, peaceful places until a belligerent country probably of Indo-European descent invaded Europe and re-established or establish patriacal political type in all Europe.

Coming from anthropology it is believable. If it were not because of this interruption, Europe would be a peaceful place and avoid lots of headachy moments and probably that peaceful mood would be exported in the rest of the world. The earth would not be a place of violence, misery and famine as it is now. It all told in the same book Hidden Wisdom. Europe was interested in the Creator, as it was the case for HBBs in most ancient religions, the invaders were of the monotheist type, male chauvinist pig religions.

Only in the wrong side of life we would force others to adopt our view on existence. Even the Creator lets us free to make up our minds on the existence to the point that we can suicide ourselves, to the point that we can suicide ourselves (disappearance of everybody at a time) by staying away from the Creator and doing stupid mistakes. Who do they think they are to force their opinion on others?

'Decision en-thinking of be-ing or nothing at all", according to Heiddeger. It makes sense.

A BIT OF A DEFINITION: WHAT IS PSYCHOKINETIC TELEPATHY?

Before I started the research, as said in the first chapter, I did not think of putting the 2 concepts together, because I did not know if it was possible, that is if we could ask someone far way from us to do something. At that time I was not thinking of the transcendental behaviors, all I knew was we could communicate our feelings to someone else away from us, now I can specify it by adding beyond time and space. In psychology then I learned that only feelings can be communicated via telepathy, not data.

The result as I collected it reporting it may not look like psychokinetic telepathy at all, for the contents are related to the film industry, songs industry, TV and business. I reported the results, as they are, the face of soul, and where I found them. Some of us may think that there are some fault with all of them, especially the TV and film, which prompted some psychologists to say they are the source of lack of imagination in North America. I do not know that.

When I first came to America watched TV a lot and went out a lot, because I have no Family in Canada where I live. Part of the Family lives in New York. Last Saturday I called one of my brothers in New York, was trying to get me to go to New York again, the lure was some Jack Daniel, and he left for me there. After the telephone talk I asked myself if the many miles from Vancouver to New York do not count. All that to say that far away family are not HBBs we can be with on the spot and that the physical loneliness and lack of goals are why HBBs may watched TV and being in the internet too much. Nowadays, When I watch TV it is late at night and I go to bar no more, busy writing and creating my goals.

So in that way I may say it is not TV, or computers or bar that create the lack of imagination which has more to do with metaphysics, lack of goals. lack of soul.

, After a while working with the subjects, Jennifer Allan, Nadine Chanz and Victoria Spelling, telepathically, communicating our feelings, I asked them to contact me. Later again I discovered the transcendental behaviors. They are developed in previously in this book. Viewed in the context of the transcendental behaviors telepathy is quite different than what we thought it was before. It is being with someone in the incomplete life while using one of the transcendental behaviors (direct communication, experience or perception) In a DP recently Jennifer was passing in a Jeep and I was in my room, we communicated quite normally, although I was too unconscious to really understand at first that is telepathy. Last night in a DP I was talking to another woman, Victoria jump over the person to talk to me. Afterward she said to me that it was because she felt neglected another expression of telepathy. To simplify a bit more telepathy is being in incomplete life and using one or more of the 3 transcendental behaviors with someone else.

Actually the 2 DP on Victoria and Jennifer 2 of the 3 subjects of the study kind of summarize for us the definition of psychokinetic telepathy. The experience with Victoria reminds us of soul or she represented the soul by the jump she made to talk to me over the first person. Soul can be defined also by movement and transcendence is the fundamental part of its definition. With soul it is an inner experience. On the contrary the experience with Jennifer in the DP reminds us of the Creator. So Jennifer is representing the Creator that way. In other experience we have learned that the Creator is always passing, it sways as would say Heidegger. I already told the story that in a DP I saw a woman (Creator can take the form of a man passing, I tried to retain her by her hand. She took her hand away from mine abruptly and continuous her going. It cannot be stopped in its sway.

In a book called the Solar System, it is question of Kinetic energy. Just after the formation there were pounding on many parts of the planets, big rocks falling from the space on the ground and sending shock wave on intended target. That is what kinetic energy is. That period was called the cratering period, for the object hitting the ground digs big holes on impact sometimes.

This kinetic energy is about physics, still it gives and idea on its psychological counterpart and a sense of psychokinetic telepathy. Can we be in the incomplete life using TBs without it being telepathic event? Or can we be dreaming without it being a telepathic event?

Still the psychokinetic part of the research cannot be well demonstrated, for the subjects do not contact me. However it succeeds in regard to phenomenon such as appearance of unusual amount of fish and minority governments, and so on.

In psychology psychokinetic action used to call distant action, you move something without touching it; the expression is not quite appropriate for there is no distance in the sense that the transcendental behaviors as well as psychokinetic action happen beyond time and space. The person maybe sitting next to me, I may have a direct communication with her in which I ask her to do something, the conversation still takes place beyond time and space. It would be the same situation even if we were miles apart.

WHY NO CONTACT?

From 1997 to now year 2010. Why Do the Subjects not contact me? There might be a lot of reasons for that I do not know, however, without the fact, speculation goes rampant, I think of a few in the following:

1. different chronological age, they are younger than me
2. Husband or companions prevent them from doing it
3. Different countries, we live in 3 different countries
4. The desire to create children with women from 20 to 30, because of my long chronological age
5. Nadine speaks English only a little
6. In this culture it is the man who does the first step, in this case it would contrary to the purpose of the research
7. TBs are in competition with other means of communication
8. They are waiting until I earn a lot of money to be able to pay them
9. The multitude of women I have in my psyche
10. My contacts change too many times
11. Psychic bloc, the ego bloc
12. My financial situation is too down
13. Different races
14. Different skin colors
15. Different backgrounds
16. I do not have a girlfriend in CL

17. Sexual harassment by men, I have to be hashed with them, may be translated as if U am a mean person
18. Homosexual bad rapt
19. The tribunal file between Rogers Nelson and me
20. My first name change
21. The fact that I am unknown
22. "Tire à l'arc" fight with other women in the psyche
23. They think that the reason for which they would contact me is too futile
24. Telephone is the work of a secretary
25. They do not know why they do not call me
26. Last but not the least, they do not know my contacts, and in other words the task is too difficult

Chapter 10

CURRENT EVENTS

Events that occur during the writing of the book and that are relevant to the subject. The Exposition of Jessie's Affairs, Jessie married to Sandra, The Larry king Scandal, the Volcanic Eruption in Iceland, While I am Writing this Book on Psychokinetic Telepathy.

JESSIE AND SANDRA

Sometimes a woman sucCesses may put a man down, other times it may not. Sometimes we have to split, other time we have to stay together. See more on that in Relation Amoureuse. There are many ways for them to have a connection with me. The most obvious is that (Reminds me of the Film reported before the previous one: 'He sees where you sleep") I want to name my first son Alexander, same letter than my first name. And I have many Psychic friends in Hollywood; I still have a court problem with a star named Prince. I am writing this book. Consciously I would say it is not my business, still it happened. Another link is that I wrote a book called Soul Exposed, although the book is not to expose anyone life in particular, although it is rather to expose human problems, basically the getting away from our creator. Today I have learned that Sandra filed for divorce and has adopted a Child from New Orleand.

LARRY KING

His last name is a bit similar than mind and we have features of character in common. More than that I am in direct communication with almost everyone I see on TV and to whom I pay attention. Despite all he was as a mentor to me, because he is doing something I would do if I can which is marry young lady and have children with them, exactly because I have long chrono and want them to be safe in the genes side of things. I thought he was having a perfect life. When I have heard the news recently that he and his wife were having affair, I was a bit shocked. Obviously I would not want to expose them consciously, neither anyone else actually. Then I have learned the many wife he had before. True or false I was again surprised. They learn their lesson.

Married life seems to be a little bit harder for actors and actresses, human beings who are popular, given that one member of the couple may have to be away at work often. There is a lack of contact, of being together, a real problem in love relationships, which may cause a partner to look for extras.

This society becomes a society communication done almost solely with gesture. The problem with that is our feelings stay with their original energy, get out by burst which causes irrational actions. Also men are not supposed to talk about their feelings (compression of feelings, later depression), another bloc of love relationships. Any way their misdemeanors are exposed now while I am writing the book may because they want to appear in it so to pass to eternity.

Tiger and Erin

I used to have DPs in which I saw myself playing gulf, not because I ever played gulf in complete life; I play other games in that level of life. I think these DPs may be in connection with Tiger. I do not really admire men in Sport, just because they are succeeding. I am still very sensitive to homosexuality matter. What I meant to say here is that it is not about him and me rather about the research and him, although I do not know at what degree. If it were for a person like you and me, the situation with Tiger and his affairs and his wife Erin would not be known. It is such a common situation we would take it like a banal situation if not boring. However because Tiger is first in his game for sometimes, what he does takes great proportion. Again said these words about him and his wife because of the research in psychokinetic telepathy.

The Power of Empathy suggests an explanation "Sometimes the impetus to a later love affair, lovers overwhelmed and unsupported in the midst of crises reaches out for sustenance".

The Civil War in Thailand

Nathalie Glebova Canadian of Russian descent may still leave in Bankok; I was "maladroit" with her after she won the price Miss of the World a few years ago. Any way she chose to go to live with a man in Bankok instead of coming to live with me in Vancouver. Of course I do not like it but I move ahead. Apparently she is in fashion now

Let week the civil war was at a culminant point in that city. Up to here it is not really my concern, living in Canada miles away from that city. Wednesday May 19, 2010, I had very bad DPs in which I saw many men dressed bizarrely following me. I was sad and afraid. I saw them in many DPs during the night. They followed me everywhere. Sometimes I was tempted to call the police, So I had a very bad night.

THE VOLCANIC ERUPTION IN ICELAND

The lesson is cleat in this one. Europe has known 2 World Wars. In fact it seemed they have been at war since the appearance of consciousness. It is true they have made big progress there in that sense since then. There is The Euro, the unit of money used by many European countries. They are not at war against each other any more. Zchek and Slovacs separated with swiftly. Notwithstanding these factors, because of the past, it seems there is still more to do in terms of public relation in Europe, underlined by the volcanic Eruption. which is like a wake up call to keep Europeans together. And also for the rest of the world to pay more attention to Europe.

The culminant point about Iceland is that according researchers in universities of Colombia and Yale, Iceland in the cleanest place to live in the world. There was 163 countries in the analysis, Iceland ranks first in there environmental performance index (Internet, April 27, 2010). The volcanic eruption there seems to be indicating to the rest of the world where Iceland is in terms of clean air and signaling to them to do the same.

I salute the researchers efforts, but these kinds of knowledge are not knowledge in the sense that they say nothing new, proves what is known and posited in advance" I get the impression that some HBBs will complained that now they will have to relearn everything again, Nonetheless that will not be an excuse not to change.

After I came back to Canada, on July first, 2010 one strange event was that Prime Minister Harper was hitting on a drum while sitting beside the Queen of England to her Majesty's great surprise. I supposed the Prime Minister was trying to please the Canadian Indian, because they could not have been invited in the meeting or the queen did not really want to see them this time, especially after a traumatic event in Vancouver (BC) a few years ago when her majesty had to witness an Asian young woman, paralyzed, on a wheel chair after being attacked in Stanley Park.

Terrorism also seems to be a movement against the capitalist. Capitalism is not the best economic system, but it performs better than other economic arrangement in the world I salute again

Canadians for their effort in making the world a betterplace to live in. However universities churches, environmental control will not stop us from going down the drain, to disappear completely from existence, of the face of the planet, for it is the getting away from our Creator that will do it, not anything else.

Universities are necessary at least to transmit knowledge in order not to have to relearn or to reinvent or to rediscover them each time. Churches are transforming themselves. Nevertheless they cannot do anything about human being sliding away from Reality, from being able to observe it in order to ground its truth.

One or 2 days afterward, the civil war in Bankok was ended. Of course I was having this kind of nightmare in order to end the civil war there. How did it happen? I have no precise idea on that, for I am having so many problems on my own. It is very unlikely I would be preoccupied by what was happening there.

I sent two letters To President Kibaki in Nairobi in which I asked him to send me a contract saying that I help Africa to unite and that they will pay me a certain amount of money after the unification. As I waited 2 months without an answer from him. that Wednesday I decided to forget about the contract and start working about the unification again anyway. That might be why my body, my soul and my spirit have conceived that in the context I have to help Bankok, because I have decided consciously to help Africa, even though they do not seem to care about what I say or what I do. Also, the civil war there may have a link in Africa.

All these wars and calamities may be telling us that we are exposed to nature and the Supernatural, to all sort misadventures and that only by observing our Creator to set its truth we will feel safe. Since sometimes from now we are getting further and further away from Reality.

Before the arrival of the G20 (meeting of 20 nations in Toronto on July 25, 2010, there was 2 two natural events in Ontario, There were an earthquake and a Tornado. The earthquake of 5 Richter scale magnitude was felt here and there in Ontario, especially in Toronto and Ottawa, buildings were giving a good scare the Torontonians unfamiliar with Earthquake. The last time they had an earthquake

There was 20 years ago, however and fortunately there was no lost of life un July. After the Tornado which happened in mobile home area, individual were complaining about the damages caused to their houses by the twister, unfortunately for them, but fortunately in that everybody involved were safe.

Ok those things are the usual events somewhere on the earth every day. Recently there was a blast of twisters in United States, not just one. It looks like a coincidence the ones in Ontario occur just before the arrival of the State persons. In my thinking it was not a fluke, goddess or god knowing the structures of these events were telling something to the Maire of Toronto that summit would meet with violence in the street, as it effectively happened. There was damages caused by the militants, and looters in Toronto. A lady said this afternoon, that demonstration in the streets of Toronto was against capitalism in the United States of America, although I was there to visit my family from June 8th to June 16th, 2010. During the big day there was a most hotdog-eating contest during which a previous winner was the world right now, what is shown by the disappearance of the communist economic system in many countries of the world.

There were two big wars, other wars in many places of the planet. Those big wars did not solve the issue of poverty; will events like what the ones in Toronto do it? It is unlikely. I am for protestation in the sense that one is not obliged to accept everything that is presented to us. Still we need a more profound protestation; one that starts inside of us before we can takes it outside. Schools and other institutions have failed us, when many of us are in a process of integration and actualization the shape the failing institutions and schools will disappear at the same time (Read Experiencing, a theory of Psychiatry and Psychology by Alvin Mahrer for more information).

BIZARRE STORIES JULY FIRST, 2010 THE SAME CANADA DAY

A bit busy nowadays I know no bizarre stories on July fourth the USA Day, although I have nieces nephews and brothers living all over the country. The same Canada day there was a young lady from Asia in Canada only since a month, not knowing a lot of English. She had many little Canadian flags in her hands and muttering some English words The interviewer Mike MacCardle trying to help her asked some passers by to teach her English words, to say "Happy Birth Canada". Those ones were a black couple. After finishing teaching the Asian the words, the TV man asked the couple where they come from? Their answer was Memphis USA. It was strange they were teacher of Canadian culture for a moment, themselves coming from the USA.

They have a good life there in United States of America. We may suppose that many countries would like to be invaded by USA to share that good life. I agreed with the second Iraq invasion but not to go there and stay that long, just to help the country liberate itself from a dictator and killing.

CHILE

There is one more chilling event in the world right now, about 3 dozen miners are trapped under ground in Chile. They make a small whole up to them and found out that they are all alive.

What is disturbing is that they rescuers are talking about being able to get them out of their trap in 4 months. I find that part of the news very painful. I am going to do something, via the transcendental behaviors, about getting them from there sooner. I do not know if I am going to succeed.

There are so many negative events in that area, nowadays, oil spill, earthquake, mining accident, I am wandering if South America is somehow neglected by the rest of the world, even by Spain. It would be the explanation of so many negative events there, to attract our attention on the negligence from our part about there.

Today July 12, 2010 I have heard again, that a study in California according to which Parkinson is linked to lack of vitamin D (one HBB published a book in which it says that all sicknesses can be cured by vitamins). What is missing in the report is that that research study was promoting the consummation of vitamin D, which may be nothing bad in itself, but why connecting the vitamin D with the disease? If the disease had a tangible spot in the brain with all the machines at the doctors disposal nowadays the spot would be discovered. Telling what is not true about it is a good way to keep illness alive. It is not pleasant to hear the report of the results of those studies

Yesterday, August 29, 2010, I wrote the previous paragraph the previous week.) I felt moved by the event (the miners trapped below in Chile) again, a bit to my surprise for days before, there was a bit of good news about it. It was said that they might be able to free them in weeks instead of months. I assume that they would be free in one month or so, a lot better than 4 months. That is to say the wish of working with the rescuers to free them sooner works. I will continue to work with them transcendentally up to when they are on ground (Where is the previous paragraph?

THEY ARE ON GROUND ON WEDNESDAY OCTOBER 13, 2010

SURPRISED BIG NUMBER OF FISH RETURN

To the Surprise of the fishermen a big quantity of Salmon about 25 millions, are in the Fraser River this year. The news came out Tuesday Agust25, 2010 the opening day of fishing. The fishermen on TV have the biggest smile and making jokes about it, because apparently, they did not have the windfall of fish for about 10 years. The industry was barely coping with the lack of fish return last year, was in collapsing state. Everyone is happy about the big fish return, the commercial fishing as well as the sportive fishing.

Apparently again there was unusual significant amount of Fish to catch this year in UK too, as it is an international phenomenon not only about fish but also about life in general created by the research in psychokinetic telepathy.

Sakineh Mohammadi Ashtiani and Carla Bruni 30-08-2010

The conditions done to women in the world is not the best, especially in developing countries; those bad conditions can be mixed with poverty, and all sort of miseries making their situation going from bad to worst. It was in the internet that Monday of August indicated above, Sakineh Mohammadi, a woman of Iran about to be stoned or to be put to death in Iran on allegation that she slept with a man not her husband, that she had participated in the killing of her husband.

The accusation that she participated in the killing of her husband may well be a cover-up for the barbaric (I had Barbara in DP the same day) of Stoning women for affairs. However if after the real course of justice she is found guilty of that she would deserve punishment. The atmosphere is rather that they really want to stone on the flimsy excuse that she had an affair outside of marriage, according to the report in the Internet.

The other part of the negative attitude toward women in Iran is that in the government they put a negative epithet on Carla Bruni, French President's wife, Carla who had advocated in favor of the liberation of the Iranian woman. Instead of congratulating her to encourage her humanist sentiments, they called her name. It is not a surprise given the little consideration they have for women in their own country.

On Wednesday September 8, 2010 it is question in the news that the woman is liberated. Bravo to Carla, even to Iranian government for this action and bravo to the international community.

In South America recently a plane currying around 200 individuals crashed (end of August 2010). Only one person died. More things like that will come.

Be careful of your thinking it creates life around you. I notice for sometimes ago, when I am writing a book, most of the time it is as if I am programming the activities of HBBs around me (I would not dare to say around the world)". After I started to write the book I realized that there is a bit of agitation around Jennifer Aniston, Lopez and Hudson nowadays on TV.

Chapter 11

Direct Perception

WEDNESDAY AUGUST 11, 2010

1) The couple is making love.

2) I am sitting on a bench. Someone who reminds me of Janet Jackson is passing close by me, I ask her to sit close by me she does Then I rob my P between her legs (Mercida).

3) Someone invades my space twice the second time the HOB is all over me.

4) She puts the tail of her dress on top of my head (definitive), the second time I yell as a joke.

5) I am walking side by side with the woman. A man wearing a strange cloth comes and put himself between us. I take him apart and am about to push him on the floor when the experience ends. (tête chargée=crazy)

Comprehension

1. That DP was rather made on Tuesday, I was at that time in a psychic shift, meaning that the only DP I remember that day. I decided not to try to comprehend it only today.

   Can we be making love with a woman and witnessing the act at the same time? It seem to be the case in this DP, for after asking the question on the identity of the two making love, I have heard

"You are Colorado"

So the woman is someone who lives in Colorado and the man is my being. I have many psychic women who are my friends or psychic girlfriends; still I am not sure which one is living in Colorado. After one question I hear

"Mademoiselle"

I concluded that it would be Kesha. Usually Mademoiselle would mean Britney.

2. There is a bit of confusion on the Identity of this woman. At first he reminds me of Janet Jackson, my waking state suggests Avril. Of course "passing" suggests also the Creator in it sway. The Creator is not touchable, approachable, but it can take the form of a woman.

    In a direct communication I hear

    "I need Philip, clairacil, Italien loves you, Chenet, 27"

    I have already said that Italien is my brother, Philip is his son. There is a Chenet in Haiti a very bad character, but now days Chenet for me means Britney's father.

3. Before I even write a word during this analysis I hear:
    "Combat, I have you, pataugé (no advancement), J'aime masculin (I like masculinity)"
    I think this communication can be taken for an explanation of the previous DP.

    Then it continuous:

    "I love Jesus Christ; beaucoup (a lot) dinero, Fondparisien (similar to Las Vegas) me"

4. This DP looks like a couple in a ceremony of marriage. That what the dress with tail would mean. I hear

    "Winipegors" of a young boy's voice

5. The woman reminds me of Britney and the man her father. Because last night I felt a bit sad about her who may be struggling between cigarette and me. Sad because it is not easy to get rid of addiction. For health reason I cannot live with cigarette smoke.

    This morning first of all, while I washed myself in the washroom, I thought of Kesha and Lindsay meaning that they were in my DP of the night.

THURSDAY AUGUST 12, 2010

I spend the night yelling "here is the stealer, here is the stealer" After seeing some beings climbing the wall to enter into my house to steal things (Chenet, they need papirus)

Comprehension

During a direct perception we are almost unconscious, Others can take advantage of the situation, enter our inner house with intention to harm us, to prevent us from being ourselves, from creating our goals. It is why the occultist takes a lot precaution to keep away bad energy by wearing robes destined to wear uniquely during occultist sessions, it is why the priests wear a cloak. In my case I do not do those sorts of things, however, I think of a circle most mornings and most nights with daily declaration to keep beings with bad intention out of the circle, out of me, and those with good intention with me. I do not know if my measure is working though.

The biggest problem that persons with wrong intention can cause me is to drag me away from dreaming the necessary DP or taking my mind away when I try to focus on something. I was close to the hole of the metro called Sky train in Vancouver once, some one talked to me via direct communication, I came close to fall in the hole in front of an arriving train. Sometimes I am closing a work in the computer someone distracts me via direct communication and I click on no yes in the small rectangular window and lost the work I have just done.

In the indicator, Chenet may be Britney's father; papirus for writings and the person talking must have been her daughter.

FRIDAY AUGUST 13, 2010

1) I am in Voswagen with someone I do not see, a bull appears right beside us, I press on the accelerator to speed away.

2) He cuts all the hair of the woman. I get myself a baton and tell him that the next time he does such a thing I am going to beat him in the head with the baton, while I am sweeping the wood on his head.

3) The second time I appear in the house with her, she is with a young man most of the time in the living room where I am lying down on small bed. She leaves me with a child and a bunch of keys and goes out with the young man. Her father arrives and talks to me about this time when things were done differently. Some guy appears out side the house. He speaks to them through the window (Arnould).

4) Direct communication in the morning while I was in toilet with Poppy Montgomery, a person who asks me to tell her "bon appétit" and a person in Madrid. Britney herself talks to me all day via DC. She is talking to me now while I am writing these lines.

Between 2 brackets are the indicators I have just after the DP or during the time when I try to understand it.

Comprehension

1. The other person is, of course, Nadine given that she is one of the subjects of the psychokinetic telepathy research, given that she is German. I do not see her in the DP probably because of the telepathy aspect of the experience.

   The bull is the symbol of my will, because it is strong and because it symbolizes the upturn market in Anglophone communities. So the DP is telling us something about the market economy. Speeding away from the bull market does not mean that I am speeding away from the bull market, which is not here now. It does not mean either I am speeding away from my strong financial situation, it is not there either. May be Nadine or Germany is in a similar situation, but I do not know that. Or I was just too unconscious during the experience.

   The DP does not mean either that we are running away from our wills, that there is a fear of will in us or our respective societies.

2. In the Haitian culture there is the idea that the beautiful woman has long hair, expressed above all in oral stories. So it is rather the love of woman with long hair that underlined in this DP. Then it is a feature in my personality.

3. The young man is without a doubt the woman's son. and I do not necessarily know now who she is. The house may represent the one I am going to have and use as a private house. In the DP it's a wide place, with almost nothing in it The bunch, of keys reflects one of my desires to have property in the Real Estate business. There is a bit of love expressed in the DP, perhaps too blurred to be considered here.

SATURDAY AUGUST 14, 2010

1) He is walking backward, hit an obstacle and fall. I am seeing it at a distance.

2) The electrician places a thick cable in the house in order not to have to replace it before long time.

3) Victoria is sitting on a chair among others, when she sees me she scratches her head or her hair, she does not seem to be happy, then I hear ("J'aime mes chagrins" similar to I like my mostalgia).

4) L'ennemi n' écrit pas—the enemy does not write

5) Une personne arrange le cable—a person arranges the cable.

6) They give me money in changes, I am not happy with that

7) I am lying at my being's. A group of human beings arrive, enter, and sit on the floor. There are also very small kids with them who are standing up. It is as if one person has difficulty to approach me, wanting to do so her body becomes heavy or something similar (your cathedral).

Comprehension

1. I hope it is not a bad vibration toward my brothers who live in New York and other parts of the United States. I do not meet very much with the other men here. It would be a good way to separate us even more. It appears innocent, but some years ago one of my nephews, Genio, received a bullet on his ass.

   Negative vibration is not uncommon in a world of HBBs at 90% disintegrated. It is why HBBs in spiritual field of work wear a cloak of some sort to keep away the bad spirits.

   The other possible meaning to the DP is related to that I was bizarrely in a bad situation with finding a place to stay from September to the end of December 2009. I was practically on the street then. I did fall in the past in regard to that, but I got back on my feet somehow.

2. Cable may an allusion to the nervous system. It said that the body is over protective sometimes forming a kind of protective coat around the nerves, blocking that way their sensitivity. It may be one thing to which the DP alludes too.

   Reference to the so-called brain diseases, being repaired, a possibility, for in "the actual" medicine it seems there is a confusion between brain and mental diseases.

   After questioning the DP I get this answer "New chez nous" French and English rhyme—our new house.

3. As a reminder, Victoria is one of the research subjects. She would not like her nostalgia as said in the DP. According the fact that she scratches her head in the DP means rather she is

having some problem with that the research will end practically after the end of the writing of this book. She will not have my undivided attention anymore in psyche. This idea may apply to the 2 other subjects, Jennifer and Nadine, They all 3 would not contact me, you may keep the research going in order to have my undivided attention.

4. I see 2 possible meanings to it. First, if we were enemy we would not write each other; second, an actual enemy who is not writing because he or she is un-alphabetized, not knowing how to write. May be linked to the lack of physical contact in regard to the research.

   After I tried to find out who the person is in the DP, I have "Elizabeth". I cannot comment on that or I do not understand.

5. Again the theme cable appears, I am having some problem with access to internet from my computer, is there a relation between the 2(Cable internet placed on Thursday, August 26, 2010, is the DP the final cause?).

6. From sometimes, each Saturday night I watch Much Music program where they make good, cryptic, adult comment on singers and their songs. I watch also sometimes, the 30-songs-count-down. The DP is probably telling us that it is because I do not like receiving money in small changes that I do not become a singer.

   I like music and feel that I can dance all day all night, that I can wake up at 7 AM and start dancing. The main reason is that I have a heart who is beating the beat all the time. Still I cannot become a singer now for "microwave oven and chicks for free", it is a field of younger HBBs, and even at that age they also can be tossed out as nothing, a profession that can be brutal career wise. So I will stay in my field despite the huge temptation.

   Receiving money in small potions is not the problem.

7. This DP could mean a lot of things; nonetheless, the indicator kind of restrains our imagination on it. Cathedral is not an allusion to church according to me. Because in my ideas there is no church, no sectarian groups, no place for adoration either. I think that living life normally everyday, a life including the Creator is adoration enough. Churches are not necessary in that sense.

   The fact that this person cannot approach me easily in that DP suggests an attribute of the Creator and what is happening to me in the complete life situation. Even after I contacted them, nobody contacted me back in return, thinking that I am like a god, while in reality sometimes I do not even remember my name. It is detrimental to my being if my friends think of me that way, even though they are free to have their own thoughts.

Members of my own family are scared of me sometimes, probably because in some religious theories god is portrayed as warrior, the Creator is viewed as punisher.

SUNDAY AUGUST 15, 2010

1) I am going to the bank, keep looking for it without finding it. In the meantime, going there I meet a young guy who touches the back of my hair, I square with him a bit, another young man appears and pull a knife on him. A Japanese woman makes someone fall. Another person tries to sell me old equipment what prompts my being to ask him what would I do with it?

2) She is standing a few meters from where I am standing up myself. We are both close to a street facing it. Some HBBs are passing by, and the woman with me names one of them. Thinking that she wants to talk to her, I called her out-loud. The one with me is mad at me saying something like it is not a théâtre (Stephen), that I should not call the other person (Pythagoras tabernacum).

3) I am looking for one thing in a big box full of things; I am already having difficulty finding it. Then the woman facing me asks me to find hers. I do it anyway even if I am not happy with her request. A second person asks me the same thing.

4) In violent remission

5) Union sabotage

6) Less reading clientele in BC

Comprehension

1. It seems to address the international monetary question; Japan becomes the third richest country in the world after United States of America, and China. Japan was second in the field since 1967, now China is the second richest country. I have heard that at Radio Canada this morning. The Japanese girl in the DP who made someone fall speaks to the link between the DP and the international event. Is it an explanation of their fall or would they fall in the economic lather because of women? In my way of thinking woman would be a facilitator instead of a bloc, but some HBBs may believe that.

In my case I would not blame a woman for financial situation, for I am sure that I am responsible for everything that occurs in my life one way or another.

There is in that DP also question of me trying to create some money and not able to do so yet.

2. Who are these women besides me anyway? they make allusion to that the psyche is not a theatre, that it is real, that the transcendental behaviors are real. I agree with that, but who are they?

    The fist indicator in the brackets may be a reference to Stephen Harper the actual Prime Minister of Canada. If I am right he may be in trouble, that would mean he is not going to be re-elected. I hope I am wrong. I do not do partisan politic. May be the liberal will take the power again, we will see.

    The second indicator, Pythagoras (l'hypothenuse du triangle est égale au carré des 2 autres côtés= hypotenuse of the triangle is equal to the square of the 2 other sides) reminds me of Heidi who was living here, She do mathematics at a hospital not very far from this house here where am living. My interest in her wane down for a question of communication and probably lack of physical contact, love. She seems to be content with me in the psyche, but for me she looks like a zombie in there. Joke apart, I like the woman in the TBs and in complete life situation. especially when distance is not a factor. Heidi lives in the same city than me, on 15th Avenue, I live on 20th. Ave there is no reason for us to communicate via TBs only.

    The third indicator, "tabernacum" may be linked to the word tabernacle, used in Québec to express discontent. I am not sure if the problem I have with Heidi and with other women is linked to that I am no longer a church person.

    There is a bit of theatrical setting in DPs the other TBs, in psyche in general, for sometimes it is the only way to make a point understood.

    The DP point also to that event in psyche and in TBs are not considered as reality. Let's say I have a Psychic inkling about meeting a woman in the store where I am going, something that I deal with almost everyday. Because of my background idea that event in psyche are not true I lost the opportunity to meet that woman. for being unprepared. When I come back home I am not happy with myself, but it happened. Even myself I have some work to do to make sure I get rid of all negative background idea on the psychological phenomenon.

3. The DP is related to my problem in general instead of using the TBs to create my goals, many HBBs want me to create their goals. I do not mind helping, when it is detrimental to me creating my goals it is another matter. I want to Edmonton once, had an encounter with a woman there. In 2009, there were 50 millions to win at a lottery game. I heard that

a group of four women in Edmonton won it. Situations similar to that had taken place in Manitoba, in United States. I have the impression that even living place to place is for me to help other HBBs in other houses to accomplish their goals. As said above when it is detrimental to the creation of my goals I am not happy with that.

4. I thought it would be spontaneous remission as it happens some times in hospitals or in psychiatric wards. The person is there for a sickness, suddenly it is gone, no one knows why. It is a fortunate event but puzzling. If someone who is poor win a lot of money at a game, we would not be able to call that violent remission. The winner will take the money and spend it in things he wanted but unable to buy in his previous life. It is happening almost every day in the world, there is no report that someone is sick of that.

5. I am working for myself since 1991, I am not dealing with union. The Federation of Teachers, the Teachers' s College in British Columbia may have tried that (and Vancouver School Board and Richmond School Board and Delta School Board I do not Like them very much), in the end I am the only one responsible for what I create un my life. The bad guys are only the instruments

6. Less readers in British Columbia, I think it is appropriate to say less reader in the world. The trigger of that DP is that it is Monday morning (August 16, 2010) the day when I consecrate 2 hours to prepare for the publication of my books.

Is the lack of reading contributed to Western civilization decline? I do not know the answer to this question. It is true that there are a lot of books in a lot of libraries in a lot of cities. But I do not know that if the content of these books is relevant in regard to Western civilization downturn or upturn. Rationally the answer to the question would be no, for if it was yes we would not have the problem in the first place, Western civilization would not be in decline.

In the libraries there are a lot more services as important as reading.

In the churches also there are lot of services more important than praying.

MONDAY AUGUST 16, 2010

1) Adoration chameau(camel)

2) The person makes derogatory remarks about me, everybody is expecting me to retaliate (Britney, a man' s voice), but I do not do that.

3) The veil picture of a bicycle, karate provenance (perversity, shoe. BC revelation of "amour" . . . . relentless.)

4) When High-end level of solitude is

5) "Dieubéni"(The blessed god)

6) One of the stars starts to communicate with us

7) Seeing the black man driving a bus, climbing a mountain while having a newspaper in front of him that he is reading, I say out-loud for him to hear You are climbing a mountain with a stupid journal in your hand (J'aime ça). I am in another vehicle running in parallel with him.

8) First thoughts DP in which I was looking sideway which reminds of REM (rapid eye movement) and DP

Comprehension

1. It would mean that HBBs with Arabic descent are adored by the human beings in the rest of the world. May be, still I do not see the relevance of that in regard to the purpose of the book which to make it so that there is a bit more spirituality in the world. The likeness of a race by another is not wrong.

   I have a back just a little bit like a camel, so may be the DP is to cast some light on my physicality for the reader of the book.

2. I do not really know what the negative remarks are about. I have just heard a man's voice says Britney, then she whispers in my ears "Come on over". She says that to me a lot of times. Everything is real in the transcendental behaviors, there we are in the essence of things, still before acting on what is said via TBs, it is a precautionary measure to verify, like it is done in complete life situation, like it is done in the science world. The event of the Tabs occur beyond time and space the degree for misinterpretation possibility is high. She would say that to me via the TBs, but never in the complete life. I suspect an excess of spirituality there.

3. I have seen the picture of the high heal shoe in DP pointing down, recently I think that it may be saying something about British Columbia on the map it is like that shoe. Seconds ago I hear someone says, "sabotage Teenager", the shoe may be a negative vibration from women who think that I am too much after young women. Sabot is a horse foot; the shoe

can be some sabotage. It could also represents love in the name Columbia, for colombe (pigeon) is associated with love, in some cultures Shoe can be associated with soul also.

4. It is already clear to us that it is practically impossible to be alone, taking into account the psyche and especially the transcendental behaviors in it. Nevertheless psyche, TBS are in incomplete life, meaning there can be solitude in the complete life situations. Here is alluded to the successful human brings separate from the rest of us by their success. Yes it can be physically a solitary place to be. But how about all the goodies that come with the success, like a powerful financial situation, having a number of HBBs catering to the needs of the successful person.

5. I thought it would be the blessing god, according my version of creation it is ok to say a blessed god, for the Creator blesses it. There is someone name like that in one of the small villages where my parents lived, Dieubeni. He used to be big, despite the poverty there. So the god in question has to do with appetite. vitality, he knows the structure of the appetite and vitality phenomenon.

6. Last night I was thinking of Galaxy in which is the earth and human beings. I was thinking that we do not even know the structure of our own galaxy, the number of suns there are in it. that each suns in the galaxy are very far apart from each other, because if the were close to each other they would burn all the planets, it would be too hot. We are still thinking of one galaxy. How about the other galaxies? How far away the are from each other. Some Astrologers say they interpenetrate each other, they pass through each other. In other words nature is a huge thing. Nature created by the Creator that gives us an idea on the extension of the Creator, not a small being somehow.

    The DP may be saying that some stars are trying to get in touch with HBBs on Earth, or that there are some other planetary system around some other sun with living being who are trying to reach us. The way "Ovni" is described is very similar to the way we could describe the Creator. That each time we try to approach it, it displaces itself, that it changes itself in many forms, all that are ways to describe the Creator, according to my personal with It in DP. So we could say that the numerous HBBs who claim to have seen the object have really seen the Creator.

7. The DPs in this last chapter of the books are like a journal. The Soul Exposed that I wrote is not stupid. They make the link between the complete life and the incomplete life, the physical and the non-physical so they are in a context. It is what I call a life with more spirituality. The way I write this chapter is similar to the way Soul Exposed is written.

I probably meant to say to the other person (Which could be another part of me also) that he is behaving stupidly driving and reading at the same time.

Then there is the indicator which make me believed that the other driver is a woman who used to whisper to me words like that, "j'aime ça", I like that. She may be behaving stupidly while driving also in complete life.

8. How direct perception happens is already described in the book, how it is produced physically by the body, but I did not say that at that moment the eyes of the dreamer is moving rapidly in synchronization. It is what is named REM for rapid eye movement. So it is like the processing of a computer with 16 or 32 bits. That was my first thoughts after I woke up today.

TUESDAY AUGUST 17, 2010

I am asked to go fishing

Comprehension

I was about to eat small fish the following day. I already bought them; it is necessary to go fishing for them.

When I question the DP things become even less clear sometimes.

"J'aime bouillante" I like boiling means that literally, metaphorically may mean I like million of $ and that translation come from the French word bou ill ante, the sound of ill similar to y as in yahoo, that it why it said the woman is Anglophone but in TBs speaks French as if it was her mother language—and I hear my name while writing it.

"I am Nadine". As you know she is one of the subjects of the research in telepathy. J'aime fiancé" voice of another woman. She seems to be in competition with Nadine, which would be bad for the research.

"embarcadaire(not even a French word) me", it is related to boat. Nadine used to express the idea of coming to Canada, It will be possible after the publication the book. cane-a-pêche(fishing rod) like somebody with a lot time in his hands

The rest is too disorderly

WEDNESDAY AUGUST 18, 2010

1) It is like you give a fish wrap

2) I am having serious difficulty with an old man and a young guy. The old one wants to pick a fight with me. The young ones call me big and accuse me of stealing something. I told him that I never steal and that he is sick in his mind and that he is good for the psychiatric ward (come on over).

3) I see myself and some other human beings in the middle of field. I can see only the upper part of their bodies. Plants screen the remainder.

Other DPs that I do not remember

Comprehension

1. I am not sure but I think there is a wrapper with last name Fish who has a nice song in the top 10 in the "palmares" nowadays second week of August, 2010). Was it Knan?

I remember vaguely that there was a TV series, the main character wore the name Fish, in or from England.

In the news that day there was a scientific person who contested the content of the announcement made by President Obama which was that the oil disappeared from the sea in the Mexican gulf, but the science man did not have a rational explanation of what happened with the oil spilled by BP equipment in the sea. Nothing unusual in the Science, there is there no explanation for a lot of things. The scientist simply does not know what occurred in the Gulf with the sudden disappearance of the oil.

It is said in the book that not to let zeal in regard to nature makes us think that we know everything there is to know and forget the Creator at the same time. For the Creator has a plan that we are not aware of.

In a previous DP it was question of violent remission. It might as well be the explanation of the phenomenal event in the gulf, as spontaneous remission (solution) as it is the case sometimes in hospitals and psychiatric wards. I began to write about the BP event right from the start in current events. At that time I wanted to participate in finding a solution and asked the company to pay me for that. I was thinking of something like the big cover of the big pipe where the firemen take water to extinguish fire. I did not called them to tell that; still they may have picked it from my being via transcendental behaviors. I did not call because I was not satisfied with that answer. I do not know much about mysterious disappearance of the oil either, I know it might be related to the research in psychokinetic telepathy.

2. Last night after writing, I watch again a film on war and the military HBBs. The thing is when I go to the library for videos I do not have a list of videos already prepared. I only take 5 that I am allowed to take at a time without elaborated criteria of choice. It is how I watch two military films 2 nights in a row. Military human beings are linked a bit with the research in the sense that one of the first women who experienced the transcendental behaviors was the wife of Colonel Hutchison, as already said in the book. Nevertheless the military films are one reason I had negative DPs.

    The indicator contains another reason I have these kinds of direct perception. We already had this indicator, come on over, yesterday's DP that is to say that what appears to be a young man in Today DP may be a young woman, asking me again to go to her place when I do not even know where she lives. She may wants to be like Mrs. Hutchison.

    Many years ago I was going to propose to a woman, someone stole the ring I was going to give her. There is a mention of stealing in the direct perception, now we start to have the meaning of the "come on over"; it is a marriage or engagement proposal. Of course during the DP I could not have made the conclusion that the young man was a young woman let alone the engagement proposal. So much so that in the house where I am living now, the same day of the DP I was having some problem with 2 young men related to homosexual harassment. May be via TBs she is manipulating them to misbehave with me so I can acquiesce to her demand without having to go through it complete life, why I do not go.

3. I had this one in the field many times already. I do not remember the explanation I have for it. I only remember that it is linked to money I am supposed to win at the game, but I inadvertently let to someone else have or I pass to someone else. Among the DPs of yesterday I had one with a set of numbers and the word "passadobre" I did write it down in this book because I thought it was trivial. The DP today is indicating that I should not have done that. At all case the word "passadobre" indicates the passing of money to others inadvertently during DP.

    And of course the field is a reminder of the Prairies, especially Manitoba where I had a good time, and where I lived for 2 years.

THURSDAY AUGUST 19, 2010

1)   I make love to the woman

2)   The person in the vehicle joins the others in the mountain

Comprehension

1.   The woman in the DP is a mysterious event to me. I do not succeed in figuring out her identity even after questioning the DP. It could be Lindsay, Heidi, or Joanie.

I have a lot of occasions for that in complete life also, for one reason or another it did not take place, either the woman was already involved in a relationships, either because our encounter was a passing event. I am not quite interested in sexuality only. I was always not very motivated to make the final step.

I am not going to say 'I never Touched that woman" as they would say in politics, still not touching a woman that way since 1998, it is likely that My DPS are full of love session. Because the DP happens in the incomplete life situation beyond time and space, possibilities are huge.

I was looking for a mortgage via internet, one night with just a little bit of consciousness I realized that I was making love to a woman I have never heard of before. The following day the woman called me and offers to find me rhea mortgage in United States. I was more interested in finding in Vancouver. At the time if I new there were going to be an international economic crash I would accept. At all case the woman had access to me because I was looking for mortgage, and she had one to offer. We cannot say that she was allowed to access me sexually because I chose Nadine (Das Auto, a compulsion to remind me of her) for the research is more or less that way, without her consent.

I was in a similar situation with a black woman who played Las Vegas, a televised series, and with a woman in quest, an Internet matrimonial agency. I watched the series and visited the site, we have a common point, and nevertheless these kinds of transcendental sexual activities are close to rape.

The night before I was too tired to be able to write the details of the 2 DPs, but I do not like it very much making love with women I do not know even via direct perception. Our will is not always present there or so I believe.

The developing countries, a polite way to name the poor countries, such as Africa, les Antilles. Countries in South Pacific grow normal population, in the sense that none of them are about to disappear from the Earth. In Contrast the developed countries use immigration from these countries to keep their population rate stability or from the down road, and sometimes the new immigrants are guarantee of the rich countries population growth or stability are from the poor countries. Nature has a sense of equalization mysterious to us.

2. The Mountain of pilgrimage, of Moses, and so on. It reminds us also the life of HBBs the most at ease is lived rather on the mountains as Hollywood, kenskoff in Haiti. It reminds us also of Hymalaya, Everest, among the highest mountains on earth.

3. At the toilet this morning, I had Lindsay talking to me or whispering in my ears. I am sure it was her because I recognized her voice and because she said she was Lindsay. When she was in Jail, I sent her a letter of support. Now she has to stay in a Treatment house. I sent a previous letter to Lindsay I said to her that I know she has a strong sense of self. Now I am wondering if she misinterpreted the letter and if that what told her got her in trouble. You cannot be strong with an iron; the tribunals are like that, an iron. By strong sense of self I meant she should not let others determine her, turn her around like top and prevent her that way from achieving her goals, from being herself.

The treatment house is not a sure thing for her either. There they might force her to conform with all the society's rules regardless what she really is inside out. That is still a bigger sin, a bigger crime according to me, for she will not be "cured" that way. If they left her feelings running wild in the treatment centre, if they open the door to all her potentials, these potentials would come out in positive forms.

She reminds of young woman I was going out with in Montreal name Linda. She was living in Longeuil.

FRIDAY AUGUST 20, 2010

1) His or her name is Hula

2) Machete

3) The person plays the clarinet

4) Microsoft

5) My friend says that she has something to tell me, I ask her to tell it to me right away, she says that she will let me know the following day.

6) Teresa

7) The young woman tells me how much she loves me while lying near my being. I say to her that I love her too. I touch her, caress her sexual being. I have some good frenetic feelings while touching her (I assume that we continue) but the DP stops before anything like that.

Comprehension

1. Who is Hula; it looks like a name in the Arabic, Spanish, or African countries. During questioning one the compulsion I have is aligator. Last time that I saw a big alligator in the sea, it was a catastrophe about to occur in ground and in the sea, I name an Earthquake and a spill of gas.

2. The use machete mostly in Haiti to cut sugar cane. I wanted to call Genio my nephew in Haiti, at the telephone company I am told that I had to have a deposit of $200, now I do not know I will be able to call Genio anymore. There is a big sugar cane plantation in the property where my parents were born. Genio's family use to manage the company when I was there.

3. As it was done at my infancy, the clarinet may be a derogatory remark at my nose. I heard that in psyche the remark is made toward Avril also. I listen to music on Saturdays; Nowadays I listen to top 30's. There is rarely a clarinet in this kind of music, however, I also like Jazz as you know. There is clarinet in Jazz.

4. This morning before getting out of bed I received a call from Microsoft, because the previous day I thought of calling Microsoft apparently amalgamated Wit HP (Hewlet Packard in Canada, HP the company where the table computer I bought is made for a question of internet service provision.

5. Or I do not know who she is or I do not feel like naming her in this book for this moment. I have a woman whispering in my hears right now. Despite the DP I do not feel it. After a few questions to connect with something else, I have heard "I like your journal"

6. Teresa was a roommate already mentioned in the book. She behaves a bit crazily sometimes in the complete life situation. She may be portraying somebody in my life with her physical characteristics in the next DP may be.

7. Heidi is as tall as she is, but I may have other women in my psyche with the same physical feature. During or after the TBs, I can know the person's physical characteristics if I ask the questions will tell me herself, Engulfed by the experience most of the time I do not ask the questions

    Lindsay is going through a difficult time it is different case as far as she is concerned, still I have some reticence to put these women a lot in the book while they have my address or my telephone number and never called me. They may only want to be in the book.

    The Author Robert Fritz says in his book "creating" that separation is essential to relationships. It is perhaps what these women read in my mind and are applying, create an emptiness in our psychic relationships to make it exist. My physical loneliness prevents me from accepting the situation with all my heart.

    The Author speaks also of mental stimulation and physical exhaustion and insomnia. In regard to physical fatigue and mental stimulation I experience that every night. It is the reason why I see someone in DP and does not recognize him or her even after doing the comprehension part, while awake. It is that after the DP I was too tired to write all the details that would allow me to identify the person, and that during the direct perception I was very stimulated mentally. So the author's conclusion on mental stimulation and fatigue and my own dealing with direct perception coincide. Nevertheless it is another matter in regard to insomnia; I do take sleeping pills every night, still once in a while, I do have insomnia, staying awake from 4 pm and up. without mental stimulation.

SATURDAY AUGUST 21, 2010

1) They appear near my being upstairs a woman and a man. The woman salutes me she has a child who she carries at her side. The woman is of white color the child at her side has black hair. Then below I see men in front of the door of Joisila's house. I ask them what they are doing there if they are waiting to steal something out loud. (Taj Mahal)

2) In bikini on the yard of the house with more HBBS, I decide to go upstairs even though I feel very week in doing so. Inside of the house I see a Chinese man whom I do not know (I like Amalia). I tell him that I can start by strangle him and start doing that when 2 white men rush into the room. I get out and leave (Peninsula).

3) Sitting on a chair at this party, a woman comes near me, my being and makes me look afar at a person who takes our picture.

4) The child is like dead, his name is Devin

5) We need effectiveness

6) In a way success is the equivalent of a failure, in the sense that success is about the already known, corresponding to the expectation of the majority, a success with respect to expectation, a failure with respect to creation.

Comprehension

1. Joisila (may be about 204 years of chronological age by now) is my mother's sister, Joisila is alive my mother is not. Genio is almost always at her place apparently. My mother is dead when I was about 6 years of chronological age. She had already made 7 children before her death, 2 of the seven are dead also, only 5 are left. Lelio my little brother is dead last year of brain tumor.

   The indicator Taj Mahal is alluding obviously to Donald Trump place, or a nice hotel like his in India. It is not clear for me why. The original Taj Mahal hotel in India was surrounded by water this week, second of September 2010.

   Joisila (joy) may be also a metaphor for love these men may be waiting for love, They house may be a house of prostitute. I would not have any information on that. What HBBs do with their lives is not my concern, of anyone else as that, but their concern.

2. In complete life also I felt very weak during this Saturday. Since sometimes after I started recorded my direct perceptions, I am like in a big distress Friday night till about 2 PM Saturday. I visit the toilet frequently to pee, feeling and with heart palpitation sometimes. I wake up many times at night all the times to write my DP, I feel this strong weakness only on Friday going to Saturday. The only rational explanation is accumulation of fatigue of the week. For I do not work very much from Friday after 5 PM to Monday morning. Tiredness from Monday to Friday is accumulated; I feel it Friday and Saturday when I am more or less resting. It could also be because no more I drink during the week. On Friday night I do have drinks which the body constancies as if the body is in shock, Now I am having the inconstancies and by remembering that fact and by taking some measure to soften the shock.

   The house where I lived last year up to the month of September on 16th Avenue is owned by a Chinese woman. It is left for her after the death of her husband. The new owner still does not give me back money I gave her as security deposit after about a year. At the Vancouver Tenancy Branch, I waited for 6 months for a resolution with no avail. On August 4 the, m

I has a dismissal with leave to reapply although, although in the that day the time of the so called hearing the owner said that she owed me the money and that she was going to give it back to me.

Before that I rented a house from an owner who was equally Chinese person. I had difficulty paying the rent a few times on time at the beginning of the deal. However, when I started to control the situation, He painted the house and sold it. The result of that is he took more than one year to find a stable place to live and to continue the research, a whole year. I am still not totally recover from the move out last September on different perspectives, the research and stability. Imagine the research in Parapsychology has been disrupted many times against my will. It is what made me think to strangle the Chinese guy in the DP. although un complete life situation I would go the legal way as I did with the security deposit.

The indicator in the DP, Peninsula, makes me think that root of woes as described above is to be found in the fact that I was born in Haiti, a poor country according to international estimation. I can be abused.

Amalia the name I used to give to Maria in my psychic relation with her. We were living in the same house.

3. I am discontent of ma situation for not having created any goal yet and above all I feel alone physically especially during the weekend. It is why I tend to ignore women in direct perception, for some of them have my contact, none of them use it to join me, or to ask me to join them. One woman is asking me to join her only in psyche while she is showing herself on TV with a new boyfriend many times. Sometimes I wonder if they are reticent to show themselves with me. That may explain the photo taking in the third direct perception. The woman is saying that she is not afraid to show herself with my being although I do not know exactly who she is, although I would like to.

4. Devin is the son of a woman with whom I was going out in the past. It is not clear to me why he is this DP.

5. It is ok to need effectiveness, but not the one in metaphysics where the effectiveness is synonym to what can be used now, in the moment, similar to cloths sold on stores, longer period of time process can be factorized in the real effectiveness. Process by definition is associated with time, not with miracle, nor with work made "à-la-va-vite"

6. Not a direct perception

Sunday August 22, 2010

1) Class is in recess

2) "étincelles" (Sparks) Winnipeg

3) An Arabic person with a red tuque (pompom hat)(hat in pompon) on his head as if on a horse

4) the fear of a man

5) I am at a house or a building; there are men and women inside. A woman asks me Where do you live? I tell her that I do not know the address of the place where I am. She says then, "Please write it down".

6) The young man says something I do not understand. I tell him that if it is a threat, we will be long gone before that time.

7) The place where I appear is like a university. A woman who is passing close where I am sitting talks to me about Didier asks if she pronounces his name the right way. I am sacking myself why is she talking about Didier and something that happened once. Another man close by me that I do not see says to the woman that I am studying, meaning I am busy. While leaving she laughs and says something like I am inviting you to come to canonize me. Many other women I do not see laugh (Vancouver).

8) While walking I came close to fall in a well of water.

9) A bunch of HBBs is around. I see my father wearing a costume near an elevator, equally surrounded by a bunch of human beings, I say "my father" out loud.

10) the woman is sitting on the sidewalk wearing a white dress. I approach her and say that I recognize her face but do not remember her name. She is still wearing some kind of veil on top of her head.

Comprehension

1. The class is not an ordinary class in a school or a university, but a class in parapsychology, on psychokinetic telepathy. there is going to be a psychic shift, The writing book is close to the end. It is the reason of the recess in the direct perception. I could go on and on, having recorded all my direct perceptions since 1991. In front of me there are 855 pages

that I started only in October of last year. I have material for a lot of books. I choose to stop writing this one soon. However I will continue to work with my DPs and the 2 other transcendental behaviors, doing research in psychology, trying to make the world a bit more spiritual than it is now.

2. I let the 2 words étincelles French and Winnipeg stand because the e after c and the e after p sound the same way. That is I am telling to myself many times that if could just get a sparks, a few thousands dollars I would be able to take it from there and create all my goals. This DP 2 may be alluding to that I would be able to find the sparks in Winnipeg probably because there is a larger population of Francophone living there. I am not sure if it is the right conclusion. It could be just a mockery from a hooligan. At all cases I do not know if Winnipeg houses that many Francophone. What I know is that there is a big population of Francophone in Manitoba.

The second way to see the DP is in that I play games with which I can win the "spark". That conclusion is more appropriate with respect to this direct perception, for there is the root of win in Winnipeg.

3. Many times in DP 1 see a horse and someone on top who reminds my of Dessalines the one who gave independence to Haiti in 1804. Now the era is not to independence but to amalgamation.

The Arabic person may be one of the "Taliban commanders" Apparently where they are they can reach it only by horse. I had Ossama in a direct perception once going there by horse.

This morning on the radio I heard the Western chief commander in Afghanistan say something like he does not know when the troops there can pull out, that it may be in 2011, but he will have to make the assessment at that time. He said also that his troops are in the winning side. I would like to see peace there right now and the integration of the Talibans in the economic and political life of Afghanistan, in the reconstruction of the country if possible.

4. In another DP the man was also surrounded by a group of HBBs, a chief of state. None the less in the complete life situation, the day that happened to my being, the fear of another man, I would not deserve to live any more. Fearing another man is not my style. I have the fear of bugs, narrow space, depth, and so forth. I fear that 90% of human beings are disintegrated, but not that one, seeing my self as equal of everyone.

5. It may not be easy to get the address of another person via the transcendental behaviors for a question of privacy. Even after appearing in their house or building, I still say that I do

not know the address. In psychology in the past it was believed that only feelings could be transmitted via telepathy. I do not know the pulse on that issue nowadays. Myself I tend to think that emotion and data are transmittable as well via the TBs. Nonetheless I only discover the TBs after I started the research on psychokinetic telepathy.

6. As said before young man in DP may be a young woman in disguise. What I say to him or her reminds me of the situation on earth right now, living according to metaphysics de Hegel and Nietzsche (exacting and "presencing", re-appearing history) and forgetting the Creator. Yes we can live like that for a long time, but one day we are going to be out of steams, engulfed by matters and unable to see, to survive. Creator is reality; we are going to be out of touch with reality, lost in the clouds with nowhere to go. Life will be impossible without the knowledge needed to renew itself and which we can get only from the Creator, by observing it to ground Its truth.

7. Didier was a friend I met in a psychology class at the University of Québec in Montreal sometimes ago. He made me cares his girlfriend parts in his presence (that was an aphrodisiac for him) with my hands. It is what the woman is alluding to in the DP. I was younger chronologically speaking, still very driven by sexuality.

"I invite you to come and canonize me" reference to my long celibacy, to church. Do you know the answer? Or may be to a love session.

8. If it were a well of money I would like to fall in it. Friday August 20th, one person got himself or herself 37. 594 693.60 dollars that he won at Max a lottery game. I wish it were me who won it or at least share the prize. I want to emulate in this field in Canada and in the world for a short period of time. In Canada I would have to win around 60 millions dollars in smaller portions because there is cap on the amount one person can win at a time, in the world I do not know how much. In a short while because the amount will continue to grow, one of my "dreams in color". Falling in the well likely to be a compulsion from another hooligan in order not twin big at the game

9. The person I saw in the DP was really my father when he was alive, in the DP with human beings around him. He probably wants to remind me of the rest of the family in Laferonay. who are in dire situation right now

This morning as I was in the wash room the last Rihanna and Eminem's song going to top 10 came to my mind. What was a surprise was that Rihanna mentioned or says something about my father the same day when I have a DP on him, meaning that she can know what I am dreaming about too. The person knows us and what we are dreaming about as well. Fortunately or unfortunately the over protecting ego blocks most of the information.

My father was living with many women at a time, Rihanna may be suggesting that I can do that to with her included.

Some humanistic theorists believed that genetic factors are not determinant in one's life for the worse or the better.

10. This direct perception was prompted by a film I saw the day before "Conversation" filmed in Iran not far from Afghanistan. One of the main character is a woman who always cover her head or even her whole face because she passed herself for a man to find work.

Despite what I said to the woman in the DP I still do not know who she is, may be Kesha or Lady Gaga.

I started to be interested in Psychology since 1978, although for a living I was teaching. The book is about a research in Parapsychology(telepathy) from which I discovered many aspects of the psyche that were hiddened to us up to now, aspects I am publishing in it. They are mainly transcendental behaviors: direct communication, direct experiences and direct pereption, diirect to mean without physical device. The publication is for you to develop your inner abilities in order for you not to rely only on external power and save life on earth.

I am living now in Vancouver British Columbia Canada.